Frontispiece: Bank holiday evening at Blackpool, Lancashire and Yorkshire Railway. Return excursions await their passengers. In the background: the Blackpool Tower, and the Great Wheel under construction.

Science Museum

The Pre-Grouping Railways

Their development, and individual characters

Part 2

Christine Heap

John van Riemsdijk

London: Her Majesty's Stationery Office

Contents

List of Illustrations

Maps:

Major routes of the:

    London and South Western Railway

    Great Eastern Railway

    Great Central Railway

    Lancashire and Yorkshire Railway

    South Eastern and Chatham Railway

    London, Brighton and South Coast Railway

I L.S.W.R. Adams 7-foot 4-4-0 and train at New Milton.

II L.B.S.C.R. Stroudley 2-2-2 in original livery.

1

III G.E.R. 'Claud Hamilton' class 4-4-0- at Felixstowe.

IV L.Y.R. Aspinall 4-4-0 at speed.

V G.C.R. livery on a contemporary commercial model of 'Sir Sam Fay'.

VI S.E.C.R. livery on a contemporary commercial model Wainwright 'E' class 4-4-0.

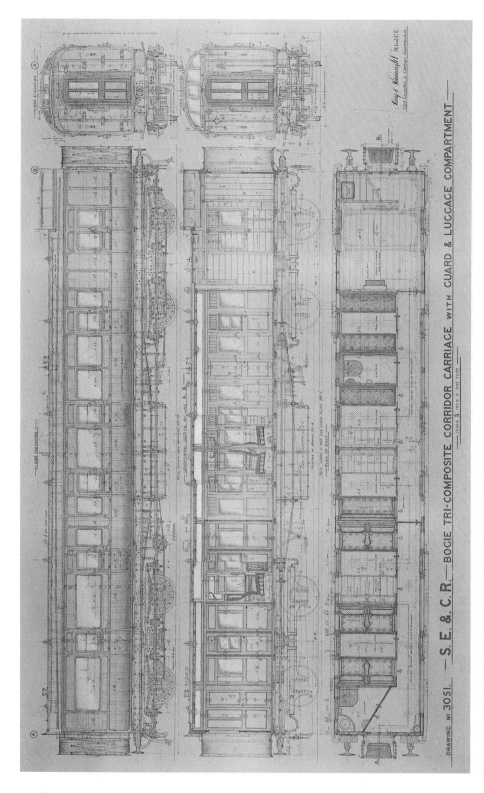

VII Tinted works drawing of one of Wainwright's S.E.C.R. carriages.

4

Major routes of the London and South Western Railway

thin lines indicate other connecting railways

The London and South Western Railway

1 Adams 'Jubilee' 0-4-2 mixed traffic locomotive, on a goods train at New Milton. The engine has been fitted with a Drummond chimney.

This was the holiday line. From Waterloo your train sped through leafy suburbs into rural England, past a few sleepy little towns. It stopped to change engines at Salisbury, and then went up and down over the folds of Dorset and Devon as far as Exeter, panting up one side of the ridges, and rushing down the other. Small market towns famous for bacon, beer and cheese went swinging past the windows of the rather old fashioned train. From Exeter you might go to Plymouth, or up to the coast of North Cornwall, while an earlier change of train might have taken you to Sidmouth or Budleigh Salterton. The guard's van, you imagined, was full of buckets and spades and the larger family pets.

If the holiday involved a sea voyage, then the train swung left at Basingstoke, preferring Winchester to Salisbury, and took you to Southampton. There you might take a railway steamer to Le Havre, or to the Channel Islands, but you might also embark on an Atlantic liner for New York (or possibly just to cross to France or Ireland in greater style).

Other possible destinations for the holiday traveller from Waterloo were Bournemouth and the Isle of Wight, and even if the holiday was literally only one day you might yet take the L.S.W.R. to Hampton Court, Richmond or Windsor.

This was also the soldiers' and sailors' line. It served Aldershot and all those other places in the area that listened to the sound of marching feet or the crackle of rifle practice. It also served Portsmouth and its surroundings, where the silent service may have been unheard but was not unseen. Waterloo was the one London terminus where, in peacetime, one could be sure of seeing members of the armed forces. In two wars, the London and South Western route played the key role among the railways in the south of England, because Southampton was the main port of embarkation of troops for France.

Waterloo was also the only London terminus with a regular service of funeral trains, though these did not leave the main station but the little private Necropolis station at the side. The London Necropolis Company had created the vast cemetary at Brookwood, where eternal slumbers were to be comfortably 'amid Surrey pines', to quote the publicity. The L.S.W.R. provided seemly and comfortable trains for the dead and their mourners. In the last war, an old L.S.W.R. tank engine very nearly interred itself at Waterloo, by falling down the big lift shaft used to lower carriages into the underground Waterloo and City Railway, popularly known as the drain. It did not survive its fall.

Like all the southern lines, the L.S.W.R. was predominantly a passenger railway, but like all railways it distributed coal. A speciality was milk traffic, carried in churns in ventilated vans, the trains having continuous brakes and running at passenger, though not express, speeds. In the not so distant days when every country station and most town ones had a goods yard and a parcels service, the L.S.W.R. managed these things rather better than most other lines, and this was because the traffic was rather light, and the distances considerable, so that slow, small wheeled goods locomotives were few in number and mixed-traffic types were preferred. They could take a turn on the holiday trains as well.

The London and South Western was a great railway, as the Brighton and Chatham lines hardly were. It had a long main line and ran Transatlantic Boat Expresses, some with sleeping cars. Its purchase and development of Southampton docks eventually won the cream of the transatlantic traffic away from Liverpool and the mighty London and North Western. Its station at Waterloo came to be the largest in London. Its carriages were painted in an unusual livery: the effect was of smoked salmon pink above the waistrail, and dark brown below, though the salmon colour was an illusion produced by buff paint and red lining. The four engineers who dominated its locomotive history were four of the most original thinkers of their times.

The first of the four was Joseph Beattie, who succeeded John Viret Gooch in 1850. He found the locomotive stock consisting mainly of 2-2-2 tender engines, some with outside cylinders, and very soon adopted the outside cylinder 2-4-0 type as his standard for all but the heaviest goods trains. Even his suburban tanks were of this arrangement, and two of these, much rebuilt, survived in service long enough to be preserved, one privately and one in the National collection. The Beattie 2-4-0s were of several different classes, and had different driving wheel sizes, the 7 ft. engines being usually used east of Salisbury and the 6 ft. 6 in. west, on passenger trains. This tradition of building express types with two wheel sizes persisted long on the L.S.W.R. The Beattie engines bore names, often rather

2 Beattie 2-4-0 express locomotive 'Shark'.

sinister ones like 'Shark', 'Styx', or 'Vulture'. They were also made more formidable in appearance by the occasional special Beattie features: two chimneys, both tall but of unequal diameter, one before the other on the short smokebox; donkey pumps on the running plates, with flywheels; crosshead pumps behind the outside cylinders and other strange excrescences.

The fact was that Beattie was a great experimenter, and various attempts at feed water heating were responsible for most of the additions. His experiments were not misguided: unsightly feed water heating equipment was later to help make French locomotives the most efficient and, for their weight, powerful in the world, but Beattie was ahead of his time. He also was one of the first to adopt the use of coal instead of coke as a fuel, and the effective and clean burning of coal presented problems which Beattie solved with further complications. All the same, his engines were outstandingly good in their time, and pointed the way to much later locomotive development.

When Joseph Beattie died in harness in 1871, his son succeeded him, but not for long, and the second of the great engineers was William Adams, the greatest of the four. When Adams joined the railway in 1878 outside cylinders were out of fashion in Britain, but, like Beattie, Adams had adopted them years before, on the North London Railway, in his second series of 4-4-0 tanks. The elimination of the crank axle made the locomotives more reliable and cheaper to build, and also allowed a slightly longer firebox for a given coupled wheelbase. Putting the cylinders outside also made the engines much easier to work on. Even though the valves and valve gear were still between the frames, there was plenty of room to stand up and work in comfort. Adams had built 4-4-0 tender engines for the Great Eastern, and he was now to build a notable series of them for the L.S.W.R., the last of which were certainly the finest and the most economical express engines in the country, in their day. He had earlier been the first to design a geometrically correct leading bogie, with spring-controlled side play, and essentially his bogie was used to the end of steam- even on electric and diesel locomotives, too.

In later life, Adams abandoned outside cylinders except for his largest engines. His earlier suburban tanks for the L.S.W.R. had been of the 4-4-0 and 4-4-2 type, a type which he also designed for the London Tilbury and Southend Railway with

3 The entry to Waterloo in 1892. Note the Adams express engine, the Beattie 2-4-0, and the diminutive four-wheeled carriages on the right.

notable success, but as the quality of steel improved he found it reasonable to build smaller engines with inside cylinders and coupled wheels at the front, even though they might be required to run fast. So he produced his 'Jubilee' class mixed traffic 0-4-2s and his two classes of 0-4-4 tank, the smaller of which lasted long in the Isle of Wight and was indeed the last four-coupled main line type (as distinct from shunters) to run on British Railways. But for his large engines, Adams, almost alone in Britain, remained faithful to outside cylinders. Each new type was an improvement on its predecessors, and he too, like Beattie, was pointing to the way the steam locomotive was to develop.

Adams retired, aged 72, in 1895, and was succeeded by Dugald Drummond, who had previously worked as locomotive engineer for the North British and Caledonian Railways. He had worked under Stroudley on the Highland, and had followed him to be works manager at Brighton on the L.B. & S.C.R. Following Stroudley principles, he had produced some outstandingly effective locomotive types, notably on the Caledonian, and was firmly wedded to the inside cylinder 4-4-0 with the slide valves placed between the cylinders. Drummond was possibly a better works manager than locomotive designer, and his greatest work for the L.S.W.R. was the creation of the large new works at Eastleigh near Southampton, in place of the old ones at Nine Elms in London.

With the benefit of hindsight it is possible to think of Drummond's L.S.W.R. locomotives as representing a reactionary phase in what had been, and was again to be, a remarkably forward-looking development, but some of them were absolutely superb machines, especially after his successor had superheated them. Valves between inside cylinders do not give such freedom for steam to enter and leave cylinders as valves placed in more spacious locations, and the later Adams engines were superior to the Drummonds in this respect, but the finest Drummond 4-4-0 of all, the quite small T9 class, had smaller cylinders than the last Adams engines, and the valves were designed with such care that they were exceedingly

10

4 Drummond 4-6-0 no. 448. An elegant but ineffective machine.

fast, and powerful out of proportion to their size. All Drummond's engines were very strongly built, with large bearing surfaces, and the successful designs lasted for as long as there was any work for them to do.

Like Beattie, Drummond had a liking for extras, and his locomotives were not always as appreciated by the running shed fitters as they were by the footplate crews. He fitted water tubes in the fireboxes, heating coils in the tenders and other gadgets, all of which were removed by his successor, Robert Urie (just as Adams had removed Beattie's specialities). He also was reluctant to adopt superheating, and eventually tried it out with his own design of steam drier, which was of little use. His attempts to move with the times and produce a 4-6-0 resulted in several types, only one of which was of any use, but even that was less useful than his best 4-4-0s. But when he did not try to innovate, Drummond was a designer of excellent locomotives: his 4-4-0 tender engines and 0-4-4 tanks were fast, reliable and smooth running, and were regarded by some as the most graceful steam locomotives ever built.

Drummond died tragically as the result of a severely scalded leg, and was succeeded in 1912 by his works manager, Robert Urie. Urie had served Drummond faithfully, but lost no time in giving practical expression to his opinions of his master's locomotives. He removed the water tubes from the fireboxes, and the heating coils from the tenders. He resited many awkwardly placed details to make the engines easier to service, and he fitted proper superheaters to most of them. The engines became even better, and though their external appearance had become a little more austere (with the removal of curved smokebox wing plates and a simpler livery) their smokeboxes extended forward, to accommodate the superheaters, added purposefulness to their already graceful lines.

Urie's own designs were completely different. His first, which appeared in 1913, was a 4-6-0 with 6 ft. driving wheels, two large outside cylinders, and a high running plate. The only thing it had in common with Drummond's engines was the solidity of its construction. This, in fact, was the later familiar British mixed traffic

5 Urie 4-6-0 no. 486. Less elegant but more effective, and the most modern-looking 4-6-0 in Britain in 1913.

4-6-0 making its first appearance, and Urie's 486 was the true progenitor of the G.W.R. 'Halls', the L.M.S. 'black fives', and the B1 class designed by Thompson for the L.N.E.R. Eleven years had to pass before Urie's hint was taken, at first on the G.W.R. by the experimental rebuild of a Churchward express engine, 'Saint Martin', with 6 ft. driving wheels. Quantity production of the 'Halls' began four years later, in 1928; 'black fives' followed in 1934 and B1s in 1942.

It is probable that Urie was inspired by the famous Prussian P8 4-6-0, which had been immeasurably improved by H. Lubken following an inauspicious start in 1907, but there was an earlier European precedent for such a locomotive on the Western Railway of France. On the L.S.W.R. some of Drummond's least successful 4-6-0s were completely rebuilt into units similar to no. 486. An express version followed in 1918, and a small wheeled one with a slightly shorter boiler, came in 1920. These last were in fact the Southern Railway's heavy goods engines, but well able to run fast with a holiday special when required. All three types were built in larger numbers by the Southern, with notable improvements to their valve gearing and smokebox arrangements; the express engines being eventually known as the 'King Arthur' class.

The early history of the London and South Western Railway Company is dominated by the recurring confrontations between it and its broad gauge neighbour the G.W.R. Beginning as the London and Southampton Railway, authorised in July 1834, the company had originally planned to build a line from London (Nine Elms) via Basingstoke and Winchester to Southampton with a branch line from Basingstoke to Bath and Bristol. Bitter hostility from the Great Western Railway, however, had soon persuaded the company to abandon its branch line and confine itself, initially at least, to its main line from London. Progress on laying this line was slow during the early years of the company's existence because the engineer, Francis Giles, was in difficulties with his contractors, but once Giles had been replaced by Joseph Locke in 1837, the line was soon completed and was opened to Basingstoke in 1839 and to Southampton in 1840. A new branch line was authorised in 1839 from Eastleigh to Gosport to serve the important town of Portsmouth and so as not to offend the sensibilities of

6 Steam 'motor train' with Drummond 2-2-0 tank locomotive.

Portsmouth citizens the London and Southampton Railway became the London and South Western.

The London terminus of the L.S.W.R., lying on the South bank of the Thames, was badly situated for connections in London and cost the company dearly in omnibus and steamer services between Vauxhall and London Bridge. To remedy this situation the line was finally extended into London in 1848 and the new station opened at Waterloo. Also in 1848 the L.S.W.R. suburban line to Windsor was opened, running through Richmond and Staines and incorporating a loop through Chiswick, Kew Bridge and Hounslow. The continuation of this line, from Staines through Ascot to join the South Eastern Railway at Wokingham, was built by an independent company in 1856 but was worked by the L.S.W.R. from its opening, giving the South Western a competing route with its main rival, the G.W.R., to Reading.

The two opponents had clashed again in 1844 over a rail connection for Newbury; the G.W.R. proposing to serve the town with a branch from its main line at Pangbourne, the L.S.W.R. countering with a proposed line from Basingstoke. William Chaplin, the L.S.W.R. chairman, who always preferred agreement to dispute, had taken the heat out of the situation by conceding the Newbury line to the broad gauge company and agreeing not to build competing L.S.W.R. lines west of Salisbury, but both sides remained suspicious of each other, and by 1846 the truce had broken down. The G.W.R. began building a broad gauge line eastwards to Hungerford and the L.S.W.R. was proposing a standard gauge line westwards to Exeter. Coming at a time when the G.W.R. was having no success with its own plans for a direct Exeter line, the L.S.W.R. scheme offered an excellent opportunity for the standard gauge company to outmanoeuvre the broad, and gain a foothold in this part of the country. Two proposals were put forward in the following year, one for a line through Basingstoke to Exeter, the other for a line from the Southampton–Dorchester branch (opened in 1847). The cost of building either extension, however, was high and in spite of constant encouragement from those who would benefit by the Exeter line, the L.S.W.R. shareholders rejected the proposals outright. Consequently it was not until 1860 that the L.S.W.R. line was opened from Basingstoke through Salisbury and Yeovil to Exeter, and then only after the initiative of Joseph Locke in resigning from the L.S.W.R. and building the

Salisbury–Yeovil section as an independent concern. The line was opened to Salisbury in 1857, to Yeovil in June 1860 and to Exeter in July 1860.

The arrival of the L.S.W.R. in Exeter brought new hope to many towns and existing railways in Devon and Cornwall seeking direct connection with London. Two North Devon railways compelled by force of circumstances to be broad gauge lines were quick to join the L.S.W.R. In 1862 the Exeter–Crediton Railway transferred its lease from the Bristol and Exeter Company to the L.S.W.R., and it was followed in 1863 by the Taw Vale line which linked Crediton with Barnstaple. New standard gauge lines were authorised to Okehampton in 1862, to Lydford in 1863 and to Launceston in 1864, while the standard gauge Launceston Bodmin and Wadebridge Junction Railway was authorised in 1864 to link Launceston to the small Bodmin and Wadebridge Railway, which had been an isolated outpost of the L.S.W.R. since its purchase in 1845. There were also plans for a line from Launceston to Truro to connect with the standard gauge West Cornwall Railway and block further extension of the broad gauge in this area, but these were abandoned as the result of a new agreement between the G.W.R., the L.S.W.R., the Bristol and Exeter and the South Devon Railways for peaceful co-existence and co-operation. With only slight modification, however, the other proposed standard gauge lines were built and eventually absorbed into the L.S.W.R. The line to Okehampton was completed in 1867 and extended to Lydford in 1874. From Meldon Junction, the Bude branch was built as far as Holsworthy in 1897 and branching from that line at Halwill Junction, the Launceston connection was opened in 1886. Wadebridge was reached in 1895, the Bude branch completed in 1898 and the line to Padstow opened in 1899. At Lydford the L.S.W.R. joined the broad gauge South Devon Railway and got Parliament to sanction the mixed gauge on the South Devon Lydford branch, so enabling L.S.W.R. trains to run into Plymouth to take full advantage of the growing passenger traffic.

Meanwhile Portsmouth had also seen improvements in its somewhat limited railway communications. Back in the 1840s the town had encouraged two new lines with London, the one running through Chichester and Brighton and owned by the London Brighton and South Coast Railway, the other running through Basingstoke, Eastleigh and Fareham, and owned by the L.S.W.R. A third line from Guildford, through Midhurst to Portsmouth had stopped short at Godalming, but was later extended by the Direct Portsmouth Railway Company to join the existing line to Portsmouth at Havant. In 1859 the L.S.W.R. gained the lease of this Portsmouth line cutting 12 miles off the journey from London to Portsmouth and bringing itself into direct conflict with the London Brighton and South Coast Railway. Determined not to allow the first L.S.W.R. train from the direct line onto their joint line to Portsmouth, the L.B. & S.C.R. chained an engine to the track and lifted some of the rails. L.S.W.R. navvies attempting to clear the line were met by L.B. & S.C.R. navvies and the 'Battle of Havant' followed. The L.S.W.R. on this occasion was forced to retreat but later in 1859 won the legal battle and gained this permanent advantage over its rival to Portsmouth.

To the west of Portsmouth, the quiet town of Bournemouth had to wait until 1884 for its link with London and its subsequent development as a holiday resort. This was because policy had tended to favour the shareholders of the company with modest dividends at the expense of the rolling stock and development of the line. Nevertheless Scott, the general manager, did not lack foresight and had been swift to lease the Somerset and Dorset railway jointly with the Midland, giving the L.S.W.R. access from Wimborne to Bath and the north, and the Midland access to the south coast and eventually Bournemouth. By 1884 Bournemouth was served by lines from Poole and Christchurch, but the route from London still ran via Ringwood on the 1847 Southampton–Dorchester line (known as Castleman's corkscrew because of its tortuous meanderings). It was Scott's successor Charles Scotter, coming from the M.S. & L. Railway, who finally remedied this situation and brought Bournemouth greatly increased prosperity by building the direct Bournemouth line from Brockenhurst in 1888.

Scotter brought a new vigour and direction to all departments of the L.S.W.R. Having been so recently involved with the M.S. & L. dock project at Grimsby, he was the first to appreciate the immense possibilities of Southampton, then a sadly declining port, and in 1892 he took over the Southampton Dock Company for the L.S.W.R. Dredging began almost at once to deepen the channels for ocean liners and by 1897 Southampton had the largest graving dock in the world. Persuaded of the many advantages of the port with its double tide, sheltered position and quayside rail facilities, the Inman line (later the American line) transferred its terminal from Liverpool as early as 1893. By 1897 at least nine other shipping lines were docking at the port and Southampton was well on the road to replacing Liverpool as the country's premier port for sailings to America. To keep abreast of liner developments. the Trafalgar Dock, 875 ft. long and 90 ft. wide was built in 1907 and enlarged to 897 ft. long and 100 ft. wide in 1910. Plans were also mooted for a new Ocean Quay and open dock to take the largest liners in the world. Alongside the ocean traffic of Southampton, the L.S.W.R. ran its own steamer services to the Channel Islands and to France. Since 1845 it had been responsible for the Channel Island mail service and had operated passenger steamers to Le Havre and St. Malo. Under Charles Scotter's direction these services were further developed and two new steamers were built for the Havre run. Services to the Isle of Wight were run from Southampton and Stokes Bay in conjunction with the London, Brighton and South Coast Railway while the purely L.S.W.R. service ran from Lymington. From the 1890's Queenstown in Southern Ireland was served by the White Star liners which called there on their way across the Atlantic.

The L.S.W.R. was above all a passenger line serving several seaside towns including Lee, Bournemouth, Swanage, Lyme Regis and Sidmouth, and many beauty spots in Devon and North Cornwall. It was also a great military line linking Portsmouth, Portland and Plymouth with Aldershot and Salisbury Plain, and a great commuter line serving Guildford, Woking, Wimbledon, Hounslow, Windsor and Ascot. Passenger services were on the whole adequate and the best trains ran on the Southampton and Bournemouth routes, and on the West Country line, where they had to compete with the G.W.R. Thus in the years immediately preceding the First World War, the fastest L.S.W.R. trains (hauled by the

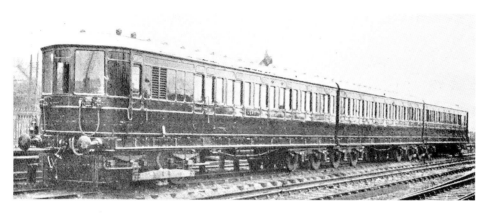

7 One of the first L.S.W.R. suburban electric trains.

Drummond L12, D14 and T9 class 4-4-0s and the T14 4-6-0s) were Waterloo to Exeter expresses, taking only 190 minutes for the 172 mile journey; and the Bournemouth express, leaving Waterloo at 4.10 p.m. and taking 120 minutes for the 108 mile run. From Plymouth, where the American line set down its London passengers before proceeding to Southampton, the L.S.W.R. ran a 4 to $4\frac{1}{2}$ hour boat express in competition with the G.W.R., until 1906 when a fatal accident on the Salisbury curve caused the South Western to reduce its speeds.

Competition from the G.W.R. also had a beneficial effect on the standard of L.S.W.R. carriage design and towards the end of the 1840s had inspired Joseph Beattie to produce 4 compartment 6 wheeled stock to match the similar G.W.R. designs. By 1861 however the L.S.W.R. was finding it necessary, on the Exeter run, to use its 2nd class coaches as 3rd class to compete with the superior Great Western stock. For special traffic, special coach designs were produced. Luxurious first class carriages, 47 ft. 6 ins. long and 8 ft. wide, were designed by W. Panter in 1893 for the American boat express (known as the 'American Eagle Express') and were joined by similar 2nd and 3rd class coaches in 1900–1. In 1921, 5 coach Tea car sets were introduced for the Bournemouth service, consisting of a brake third, pantry third, first and brake third and were equipped to serve not only tea but also egg dishes and grills. Up to that time few restaurant cars and few corridor coaches had been used by the L.S.W.R. Bogie coaches however had been introduced on the line in 1881 and by the early 1900s were usual on all L.S.W.R. trains, apart from some workmen's trains and some Ascot race specials.

The commuter services of the L.S.W.R. had been developed in competition with the L.B. & S.C.R. and the S.E.R., and encouraged since 1852 by the introduction of season tickets for all passengers and by publicity campaigns declaring the L.S.W.R. lines to lie in the healthiest and most attractive areas of London. By 1910 the company was carrying almost as much suburban traffic as the G.E.R. at Liverpool Street. To maintain the standard of services into London the decision to electrify the most crowded lines was taken in 1913 by the new general manager, Herbert Walker, and his locomotive engineer, Robert Urie. In spite of the outbreak of war the work went ahead and by 1915 the Waterloo, Wandsworth, East Putney and Wimbledon line was electrified on the distinctive L.S.W.R. system employing three rails and using the running rails as returns. The Waterloo, New Malden, Kingston and Barnes Loop was electrified in 1916 and other lines followed to become the basis of the Southern Railway's extensive electric services.

Consisting mainly of cattle, coal, timber, and agricultural produce, the L.S.W.R. goods trade had been greatly developed by Archibald Scott as a result of agreements with other companies for handling through traffic to and from the south coast. These links with the north-south trunk routes, so important to the L.S.W.R., were improved in 1919 by the construction of a new marshalling yard at Feltham on the Windsor-Reading line. This large yard, replacing several smaller ones, was ideally situated for the interchange of traffic between the L.S.W.R., the L.N.W.R., the Midland, the G.C.R., the G.N.R. and the G.E.R., via the various cross-London connections, and avoided the necessity of working 'foreign' freight trains over the L.S.W.R. main lines.

At the grouping, Urie's engines certainly looked more modern than any others in the country except for the most recent Great Northern designs and the smaller modern engines of the S.E.C.R. The whole locomotive stock was very good indeed and there was already the beginning of suburban electrification, on the third rail, low voltage system which the Southern was to develop so extensively and which still serves the region so effectively. In other respects, the L.S.W.R. was rather run down. It had borne a disproportionate burden during the war and had had little opportunity to maintain its permanent way and civil engineering works. But it had done a great deal of modernisation at Southampton docks; it had completely transformed Waterloo station from a confusing mass of apparently separate termini into a single, vast but logical entity; and at Eastleigh the main works were splendidly equipped. If was fitting, therefore, that the chairman and the general manager, Sir Hugh Drummond and Sir Herbert Walker, should be the first holders of those positions on the Southern Railway, when it absorbed the L.S.W.R. in 1923.

Major routes of the Great Eastern Railway

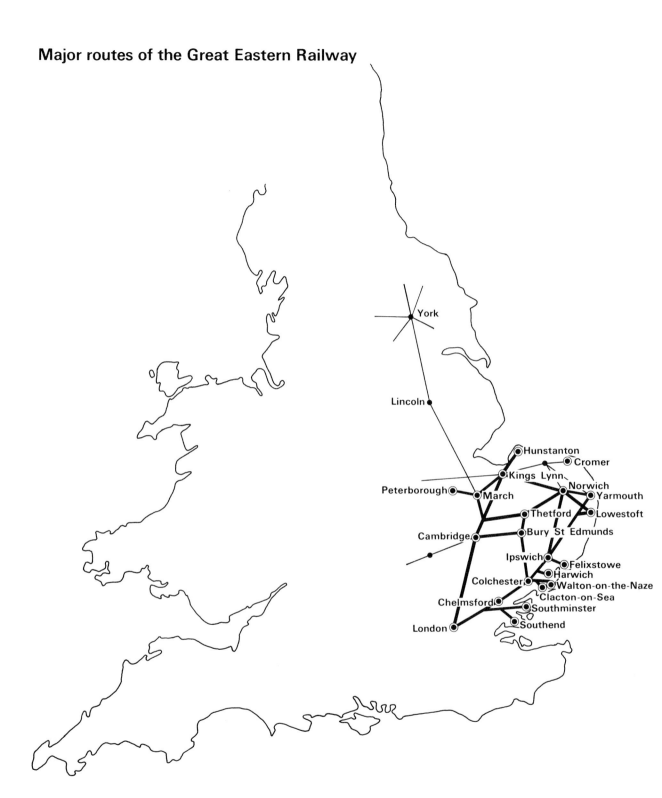

York

Lincoln

Hunstanton

Cromer

Kings Lynn

Norwich

Peterborough

March

Yarmouth

Thetford

Lowestoft

Cambridge

Bury St Edmunds

Ipswich

Felixstowe

Harwich

Colchester

Walton-on-the-Naze

Clacton-on-Sea

Chelmsford

Southminster

London

Southend

thin lines indicate other connecting railways

The Great Eastern Railway

8 Hertford East Station, a typical G.E.R. market town station in East Anglian Dutch style.

The companies which amalgamated to form the London and North Eastern Railway in 1923 did not lose their individuality as rapidly as those entering the other groups. This was partly because the L.N.E.R. management contained a fair number of country gentlemen who understood local loyalties and saw no reason to antagonise staff or customers by disregarding them. It was also because the railways absorbed were generally well run but very short of money. Thus it was that the Great Eastern was still recognizably the Great Eastern well into the 1950s.

The particular character of this railway was perhaps that it offered the widest contrasts. No railway branch line was more rural than some of those in East Anglia, and no railway in the world more urban than that which left Liverpool Street, and carried over 100 million passengers every year in and out of London, all in steam trains. The seaside excursion trains often included six-wheeled carriages, even in L.N.E.R. days, while the continental boat trains were always luxurious by the standards of their time, and at an early date made better provision for eating en route—not only for the first class passengers—than could be found elsewhere. The locomotives were either small, square, and very plain, with unadorned stovepipe chimneys and tiny draughty cabs for their crews; or else they were apparently large, highly ornamental, and provided with palatial cabs of such a size that some firemen complained that the coal 'caught cold on the way from the tender to the firebox'.

9 A G.E.R. Sinclair single driver in the 1860s. Obviously a special train, with the passengers and staff posing for the photographer.

The rural side of the Great Eastern included branches where the rails were invisible, even from the locomotive, at certain times of the year, because the grasses and wild plants had completely colonised the ballast of the track. There was at least one where even the smallest normal tank locomotives were too heavy unless they ran with their side tanks empty, so they ran with old tenders from engines of long ago, to spread the weight along the frail permanent way. It was also on the former Great Eastern that British Railways persisted longest with the once common practice of using horses for shunting wagons.

The complex history of the company resulted in many branch lines of superior quality, and the invitation to 'change here for Saffron Walden' or for Hertford, Buntingford, Newmarket or one of countless other peaceful little towns was extended at almost every main line stop. Hertford, indeed, enjoyed for a time the special distinction of having five coaches 'slipped' off the back of an express from Liverpool Street. While the main train thundered on, those five coaches drifted to rest in Broxbourne Station, to be picked up by another locomotive and briskly conducted to the County Town.

The grandest train was the evening 'Hook of Holland Continental' and no G.E.R. locomotives were larger, lovelier, or harder worked than the 1500 class 4-6-0s that worked it. They were in fact quite small locomotives of the type, weighing no more than 102 tons with their tenders. A vivid memory is of putting one's head out of the window as the heavy train roared up Brentwood bank. Looking up, against the dark sky the streaming exhaust glowed a fiery red with the glare from the firebox, the door of which stayed open as the fireman ceaselessly piled coal into the furnace.

The most intensive steam operated suburban service in the world was to be seen in action in Liverpool Street Station in London. A careful replanning of schedules and track layout was carried out immediately after the First World War by Sir Henry Thornton, who had joined the Great Eastern from the Long Island Railroad in the United States just before the war. By providing short locomotive 'refuges' at the outer ends of the platforms, it was made possible for a waiting locomotive to attach itself immediately to the outer end of an arriving train, while the passengers detrained and those wishing to make the outward journey boarded. For them things were made simpler by platform markings telling them where the

10 Holden 0-6-0T on 'Jazz' train, c. 1921.

various classes of accommodation would be found, while the first and second class carriages bore yellow and blue stripes respectively, above the windows, for quick identification.

These trains were worked by very small locomotives, mostly 0-6-0 shunting tanks of the type of which one is preserved in the National Railway Museum at York. The extraordinary vigour with which these little engines rushed their heavy trains up Bethnal Green bank out of the station, and then rocked from side to side at the numerous junctions of the intricate suburban network, on their way to Enfield, Epping, Romford and other north eastern suburbs—this was unforgettable and quite unlike the proceedings on any other British suburban railway. It was perhaps a little like the elevated railways of New York or Chicago, where similarly small locomotives, but with lighter trains, achieved some remarkable speeds between very close stops. But those trains mostly ran without the benefit of signals. The Westinghouse air brake was essential to both systems, for brisk operation demands hard braking at the last possible moment.

The 'Jazz' service, as this was called, was the final stage in a long process of increasing the passenger capacity of suburban services. As far back as 1864, Parliament had laid upon the railway the duty to carry workmen from Edmonton and Walthamstow at a return fare of twopence. This ensured a large, if unprofitable traffic, and the railway's subsequent policy of encouraging suburban development presented it with a growing problem which it always tackled with ingenuity and optimism. At the turn of the century old suburban carriages were slit longitudinally down the middle and widened to take six persons across the width, instead of five, by splicing in a thin central section. The small tank engines used at the period were mostly four-coupled: 0-4-4 and 2-4-2 types. These trains could accelerate to 20 m.p.h. in 30 seconds, but the proposers of a new electric railway in the Great Eastern area maintained that with the newer form of motive power 30 m.p.h. could be reached in the time. This challenge was met in a spectacular style.

Stratford Works turned out the 'Decapod' at the end of 1902. It was the ultimate in steam suburban tank engines, and its accelerative power, like the evaporative capacity of its boiler, was never surpassed in any British locomotive for such service. It had ten wheels, all coupled, and three cylinders, but its weight at 80 tons was too great to allow much water capacity. It was not built for normal

11 Widening carriages at Stratford works, to seat six a side.

service at all—the underline bridges and much of the track itself were unsuitable at that time for anything so heavy—but simply to prove a point. It did this by accelerating a 315 ton train to 30 m.p.h. in just under 30 seconds, along a piece of the line at Chadwell Heath which had been specially equipped with an ingenious electrical timing device, which recorded not just the final speed and time but also the smooth progress of the acceleration.

The 'Decapod' effectively killed the proposals for an electric railway, and half a century had to elapse before much of the old G.E.R. suburban routes was electrified. This story pinpoints the importance of Stratford Works, which were founded by Hudson, the Railway King, and opened in 1848. Unlike many railways the G.E.R. built almost all its own locomotives, carriages and wagons, as well as many other things needed by the railway. It even had its own plant for producing the gas used to light the carriages and the residues from this plant were for a time used to fire the locomotives. Stratford, being in London, was also the site of the 'home' shed of the engines used in the intensive suburban services, and the work done on the engines in the shed, and in the Works alongside, was an essential part of the success of these operations. Some railways—the North Eastern was an example—never worked their locomotives intensively, or even particularly hard when they were on the road with a train. Those that did—especially the Great Eastern and the London and North Western—had developed large, well equipped workshops with large staffs of unusual ability.

The locomotive engineers of this railway succeeded one another rapidly until 1885, when James Holden was appointed. All the same, among Holden's predecessors were at least four men of distinction. Robert Sinclair, appointed in

12 Stratford works in 1864. Among the new Sinclair engines under construction are Gooch 2-4-0s and an unidentified engine with a 'haystack' firebox.

1856, came from the Caledonian, but also acted as consultant to railways abroad and originated the 2-4-2 tender engine with outside cylinders—a type which became extremely numerous and was long associated with French railways. For the Great Eastern he built something similar, but a tank engine, and also produced a very successful 2-2-2 with outside cylinders, much like the contemporary products of Crewe.

Samuel Waite Johnson, who left for the Midland in 1873 after seven years at Stratford, produced some characteristically elegant locomotives which were obviously the forerunners of his Midland designs, but his successor, William Adams, did more than anyone else to establish the look of Great Eastern locomotives—a look which all but the largest were to retain right to the end. His engines were plain and well proportioned, with stovepipe chimneys and airy, not to say draughty cabs. In his five years at Stratford, Adams produced nothing very notable, but he did a great deal of successful modernising of the older engines, and at the end designed the first British 2-6-0. Unfortunately his successor, Massey Bromley, changed the design in some respects, and these engines were not a success, but the first of them bore the name 'Mogul', which has been the international nickname for this wheel arrangement ever since. When Adams left for the London and South Western he was succeeded by T. W. Worsdell, who in four years designed an outstanding 0-6-0 goods engine, several very good types of tank locomotive, and his first compounds, before leaving for the North Eastern in 1885.

With such a history before him, it is not surprising that James Holden devoted his 23 years in the job to a large measure of standardisation. There was much that was excellent in the designs that Adams and Worsdell had left behind them, and Holden's engines, at least until 1900, showed no conspicuous difference.

But in fact some remarkable things were being achieved. Five classes shared

23

13 Holden 7 ft. 2-4-0, oil-fired, ready to work a Royal train.

the same boiler and cylinders: 2-2-2, 0-6-0, 2-4-0 with 7 ft. driving wheels, 2-4-0 and 2-4-2T both with 5 ft. 8 ins. driving wheels. Of these classes the 2-2-2 disappeared very quickly, but the driving wheels were almost the only parts which could not be used as spares for the other types. The small wheeled 2-4-0s lasted very long, some almost to the end of steam traction on British Railways, and one of these, too, is preserved in the National Railway Museum.

Holden's later designs were mainly due to F. V. Russell, his chief draughtsman. The 4-4-0 which appeared in 1900 and bore the name 'Claud Hamilton' may indeed have owed more than its name to that great and aristocratic railway chairman, who presided over the affairs of the company from 1893 till the end of the G.E.R.'s independent existence. Hamilton attached great importance to the appearance of his company's trains, and he may well have suggested a departure from the austere legacy of Adams. The result was highly ornamental. A lipped chimney with a polished top replaced the stovepipe, a steel ring shone upon the smokebox door, a large cab with brass framed sidewindows and white roof suggested luxury for the driver and fireman, and deep coupling rod splashers were provided with brass rimmed openings, not just for access to the crankpins, but along the whole length. Enlarged by degrees, and eventually mostly superheated, the 'Claud Hamilton' 4-4-0s were always among the most powerful engines of their type and weight in the country. Their performances, especially on the 'Norfolk Coast Express', were at one time celebrated and only regularly surpassed after nationalisation, when the 'Britannia' Pacifics came into service, though the 4-6-0 types of later G.E.R. and L.N.E.R. days were able to show greater power when the need arose.

24

14 G.E.R. 1500 class 4-6-0 as built for the L.N.E.R. after grouping, with coupling rod valances removed and Lentz poppet valve gear.

The 'Claud Hamilton' class followed a last unsuccessful attempt to work the best expresses with single drivers. Holden's last singles were 4-2-2s with 7 ft. driving wheels, and a layout much like that of Johnson's successful singles on the Midland. Ten of these engines appeared in 1898. This was during the revival of the single driver brought about by the development of steam sanding gear to help the grip of the wheels on the rails when starting. These last singles were capable of good performances, but it soon became apparent that there were no trains on the Great Eastern to which they were really suited and they hardly lasted a decade. It is strange to reflect that four years after their introduction, Holden was supervising F. V. Russell in the design of the ten coupled tank engine!

Two last locomotive types must be mentioned. The 1500 class 4-6-0s first appeared in 1911, when Holden's son, Stephen, had succeeded his father. Of all the British 4-6-0s with two inside cylinders only, these were by far the most successful. They had a life span of some 50 years, during which some were built by the L.N.E.R. and many were enlarged. These 80 engines were valuable and well liked by the crews wherever they went. They rode beautifully and put out power out of proportion to their size, even when old and in poor condition. They are among the few classes that really deserve to be considered great.

At the end of 1914 the first two Great Eastern 0-6-2 tanks appeared. Eventually there were over 100 of them, but most of these were built after the grouping by the L.N.E.R. Though quite light (just over 60 tons) and with small wheels, they were remarkably speedy and powerful engines. In later years they were used on other parts of the L.N.E.R. system and were capable of equalling the work of much larger machines, such as the Great Central 4-6-2 tanks.

Before entering the detailed history of the system, something should be said about Great Eastern stations. Many of these were built by the previous smaller companies, but regardless of their origin, they all, except for the London ones, had a marked East Anglian flavour. They tended to be either simple weatherboard structures, or else of brick and stone with a Dutch look about them. Many are now listed buildings, and it is arguable that the Great Eastern could show the highest average of architectural merit of any of the pregrouping railways, though without a single really grand building.

Liverpool Street, the London terminus of the major routes, still stands, though threatened with redevelopment. It is a structure which commands affection rather

15 G.E.R. restaurant car interior: luxury for the continental traveller.

than admiration, and one which could be awe-inspiring when smoke and steam wreathed its columns and meandering footbridges. As one of the gateways by which continental visitors entered the United Kingdom it presented a picture of Victorian engineering and London fog which could be thoroughly enjoyed, and the Great Eastern Hotel, thanks no doubt to generations of Dutch visitors, was one of the few places in London where the coffee could be recommended. This very large station was where the 100 million passengers per year were handled, but there was another Great Eastern terminus in the City: Fenchurch Street. That had only four platforms, and most of its traffic was that of the London Tilbury and Southend line; a small railway which, with 79 miles of route as against the G.E.R.'s 1200, yet handled 30 million passengers per year.

It was a great misfortune for the G.E.R. that this prosperous railway was bought by the Midland. The Tilbury line not only offered the quicker route to Southend. It also served the dock area and handled some cross channel as well as ocean traffic. Fortunately for the G.E.R., the Midland contented itself with enjoying the revenue and never seems to have viewed the L.T.S. section as anything but a local suburban railway, rather detached from the main system, and without development potential.

To the enthusiast, the beautifully proportioned and ornately painted Tilbury locomotives were spoilt by red paint and ungainly Midland chimneys, domes and smokebox doors. Had the Great Eastern taken them over, the rich royal blue locomotive livery, lined in red and black possibly with a white cab roof, would have become them beautifully, while the varnished teak carriages would have remained as they were—and the Great Eastern would have become more prosperous as well as greater.

The Great Eastern Railway Company evolved from the Eastern Counties Railway. Through the financial troubles of neighbouring lines the E.C.R., although itself not flourishing, had been able to extend its influence throughout East Anglia. It had leased the Northern and Eastern Railway in 1842, bought the Wisbech, St. Ives and Cambridge, and the Newmarket Railways in 1845 and 1852 respectively, begun operating the Norfolk and the East Anglian Railways in 1848 and 1852, and absorbed the Eastern Union Railway in 1854. The Act of 1862 by which the Great Eastern Railway was constituted simply confirmed the existing situation by amalgamating the E.C.R., the East Anglian, the Newmarket, the E.U.R. and the Norfolk Railways with the East Suffolk and other smaller lines while at the same time providing for the continued lease of the Northern and Eastern. It thereby gave the G.E.R. main lines from London to Ipswich and Norwich with branches to Lowestoft and Yarmouth; and from London to Cambridge with branches to King's Lynn, Norwich and Yarmouth. Other lines ran from Wymondham to Dereham, Fakenham and Wells, from King's Lynn to Dereham and from Cambridge to Huntingdon, Newmarket and Bury St. Edmunds.

From the outset the railways in East Anglia had experienced considerable difficulty in remaining solvent. Most had seen delays in building their lines through lack of funds and few had had the amount of traffic at first envisaged. The E.C.R. although authorised to build a line from London to Ipswich, Norwich and Yarmouth got no further than Colchester, arriving there on its own peculiar 5 ft. gauge in 1843.

The Northern and Eastern, with a line planned from London to Cambridge in 1836, had only reached Bishops Stortford by 1843 (also on the 5 ft. gauge) and could not progress to Newport and Cambridge until leased by the E.C.R. Both railways had the additional expense of converting their gauge from 5 ft. to the standard 4 ft $8\frac{1}{2}$ ins. in 1844 and by the following year finances were so bad that George Hudson, the 'Railway King' was called in by the shareholders to restore confidence in the company. He set about his task by paying high dividends and proposing several ambitious schemes, only a few of which materialised. In 1847 the Cambridge—St. Ives line was opened in conjunction with the East Anglian's St. Ives—Huntingdon line, and the Stratford to North Woolwich line was acquired giving the E.C.R. an outlet to the river Thames, useful to the Arsenal workers and popular with the public. But the financial state of the E.C.R. continued to decline and Hudson having failed in his task was deposed in 1849.

Other companies had little more success. The Eastern Union Railway, with its line from Ipswich to Colchester opened in 1846, absorbed the Ipswich, Bury St. Edmunds line in 1846, built branch lines to Hadleigh and Norwich in 1847 and 1849 but ended in serious difficulties due in part to the rivalry of the E.C.R. By 1854 a reorganisation of the company was necessary and the E.C.R. seized its opportunity to gain control. The East Anglian Railway had lines from King's Lynn to

Ely and King's Lynn to Dereham, St. Ives and Huntingdon, but by 1850 was bankrupt and in the hands of the Official Receiver. The Newmarket Railway opened its line from Chesterford to Newmarket in 1848 but was unable to complete its Cambridge extension until 1851. Lastly, the Norfolk Railway, formed by the Norwich and Yarmouth of 1844 and the Norwich and Brandon of 1845, was taken over by the E.C.R. in 1858 ostensibly to save it from financial perdition.

Not surprisingly, considering this background, the G.E.R. itself was soon in serious financial difficulties. Faced with the general economic recession of 1867 the company went bankrupt. Some of its rolling stock was claimed by angry creditors and locomotives appeared with brass plates attached declaring them on hire to the G.E.R. by courtesy of the various shareholders. Drastic steps were necessary to rationalise the financial affairs of the company and Samuel Laing MP, former finance minister of India, joining the G.E.R. board of directors, was the man to take them. His first move was to raise £3 million of debenture stock on terms that would give the shareholders more control over the company's affairs and he, together with Lord Cranborne, elected chairman of the company in 1868, soon succeeded in restoring confidence in the viability of the G.E.R. Lord Cranborne, as the Marquess of Salisbury, was later prime minister.

Contributing to the difficulties faced by the railways in East Anglia was their lack of heavy goods traffic. The boots of Norwich, rifles of Enfield, fish from the Yarmouth and Lowestoft docks and the foodstuffs of the eastern counties could not entirely compensate for the very small traffic in coal and manufactures. Both the E.C.R. and the G.E.R. realising this, had made constant attempts to gain access to the South Yorkshire–London coal trade but had seen their plans defeated by the Great Northern Railway. By 1866 the G.N.R. was prepared to grant running powers to the Great Eastern for coal traffic from Spalding to Gainsborough but with the basic problem thus only partially solved there were to be recurring conflicts between the two companies until 1879 when the Huntingdon to Doncaster line via March, Spalding, Lincoln and Gainsborough was vested jointly in the G.N.R. and the G.E.R.

Other significant developments in the G.E.R. track network were the leasing of the London and Blackwall Railway in 1866, giving the G.E.R. docking facilities and shipping interests in the City area: the opening of the King's Lynn to Hunstanton extension in 1862 (providing a through route to Wolferton near Sandringham House which eventually led to Royal Patronage of this particular route) and the extension of the G.E.R. London line from Bishopsgate to Liverpool Street in 1874–5. 1865 had seen the opening of the Shelford to Sudbury line and 1867 the opening of the Colchester, Weeley and Walton-on-the-Naze branch. Between 1875 and 1883 Thetford was linked with Swaffham and Bury St. Edmunds and in 1881 the East Norfolk line from Whitlingham Junction to Cromer was vested in the G.E.R.

This gave the company an almost complete monopoly of rail transport within East Anglia. In the north the only major intrusion was that of the Midland and Great Northern from Saxby, which operated the Spalding, King's Lynn and Yarmouth line with its branches to Sheringham, Cromer and Norwich as a joint railway from 1889 and 1893. Relations between the two companies and the

G.E.R. were on the whole friendly, but as if to gain compensation for the invasion the G.E.R. had interests in the construction of two lines in central England, from Chesterfield to Lincoln in 1896–8 and the Sheffield District Railway of 1900, both of which augmented the G.E.R. goods trade, the one with coal from Derbyshire pits, the other with steel from the Sheffield area. In the South, the London, Tilbury and Southend Railway limited G.E.R. access to one of the richest parts of East Anglia, and its purchase by the Midland in 1912 was a major defeat for the G.E.R. board.

With its lines serving the university town of Cambridge, the race course of Newmarket and many coastal resorts G.E.R. passenger traffic was heavy, particularly during the summer months. Trains ran to Norwich and the coast via Cambridge and Ipswich and friendly rivalry between the two routes had brought Cambridge within $1\frac{1}{2}$ hours of London by 1866. The Newmarket races demanded special trains; from the end of the 19th century, new through expresses, famous in their own day, were introduced to deal with the seasonal holiday traffic. In 1897 came the 'Cromer Express' later known as the 'Norfolk Coast Express' which ran from London to Cromer in 2 hours 35 minutes, and in 1904 the non-stop Yarmouth and Lowestoft trains began operating between London and the sea, taking only $2\frac{1}{2}$ hours for the journey. In conjunction with the G.N.R. and the N.E.R. through services were introduced between Liverpool Street and Doncaster in 1882, between the Harwich steamers and Doncaster in 1885 (this train being known as the 'North Country Continental') and between Liverpool Street and York over the famous 'Cathedral route' via Ely and Lincoln in 1892.

From Harwich, a well-placed port on the rivers Orwell and Stour, the G.E.R. had operated its own Continental steamer services since 1863, one steamer each week leaving Harwich for Rotterdam in that year. This was followed by a similar service to Antwerp in 1864 and after the construction of the new Parkeston Quay (opened in 1882 and named after the company chairman Charles H. Parkes) additional services were introduced to Hamburg in 1884 and to Gothenburg in 1910. The importance of Harwich was further enhanced in 1898 when the G.E.R. regained the right to carry mail to and from Holland.

Although coaching stock was never one of the strong points of the G.E.R. (they were still running six wheel non-corridor stock in 1923) boat trains were among their best and it was for the Liverpool Street–Hook of Holland boat express that the first G.E.R. all-corridor train was introduced in 1904. Consisting of thirteen carriages it was also the first G.E.R. train to be steam heated throughout and as such added considerably to the high reputation of the Continental services. A similar train for the 'North Country Continental' was produced in 1906. Together with the Midland Railway, the G.E.R. was in the forefront with its enlightened passenger-carrying policies. In 1870 it had abolished supplementary express fares on all but the boat trains and in 1872 had allowed third class passengers on all its trains. Then in 1891, with the introduction of restaurant cars on the 'North Country Continental', came the startling innovation of allowing third class passengers dining facilities. Restaurant cars were introduced on the Liverpool Street–Cromer and Yarmouth route in 1899 and shortly afterwards on the Southend, Clacton, Hunstanton,

Harwich and Norwich routes. The restaurant facilities consisted of three carriages vestibuled together but cut off from the rest of the train and passengers desiring meals had to travel in their respective dining cars for the whole journey. The 55 ft. kitchen car occupied the centre position with a 55 ft. third class car seating 52 passengers on one side and a 48 ft. first class car seating 20 passengers on the other side. Second class fares on all but the boat trains and commuter services were abolished by the G.E.R. in 1893.

The Great Eastern, then, was a progressive, well-run railway, with an air of frugality about all but its most publicised services. It was a railway with a style, simple and visually pleasing on the branch lines, elegant and efficient on the main lines, grandiose in nothing and squalid in nothing. It was run in a very real sense by Lord Claud Hamilton, and the large staff were loyal and capable—tough cockneys and crafty countrymen. Its technical traditions were excellent and many of its locomotives survived the whole L.N.E.R. period and lasted into the final years of steam. It is remembered with great affection, even by many born after it had ceased in theory to exist, because its character so long outlived its absorption into the larger group.

Readers of this

JUBILEE ISSUE

ARE

Invited to consider

THE

Facilities Afforded

BY THE

Great Central Railway

Prompt Collection and Delivery
Quick Dispatch and Shipment
OF ALL KINDS OF MERCHANDISE.

IMMINGHAM is the great Coal Port.

Ships can bunker at any state of the tide.

" PER RAIL " A well written
and illustrated publication, containing three useful Maps, will
be sent to bona-fide Traders on
application to Publicity Dept.,
216, Marylebone Road, London,
N.W.

SAM FAY, General Manager.

16 G.C.R. magazine publicity, 1914. The Locomotive is no. 423 'Sir Sam Fay'

Major routes of the Great Central Railway

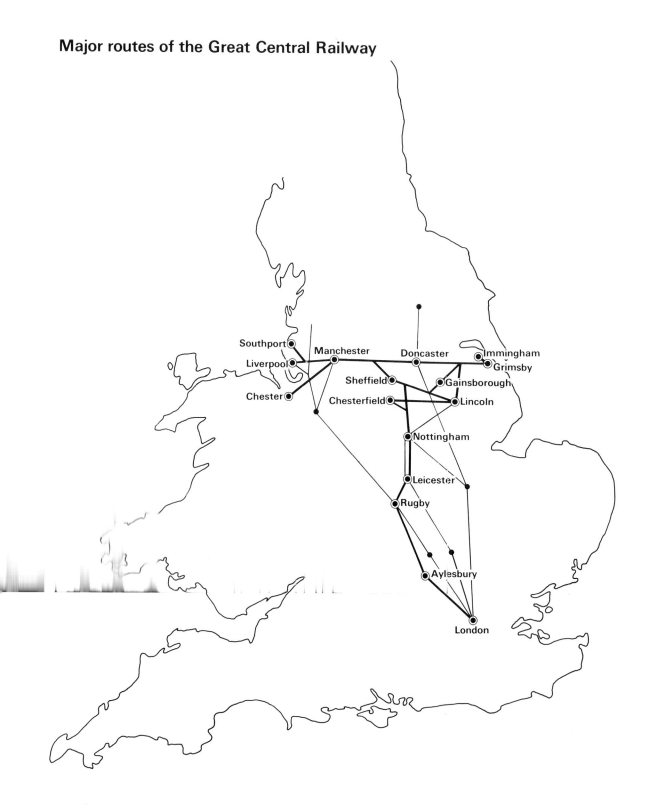

thin lines indicate other connecting railways

The Great Central Railway

17 G.C.R. A Robinson 'Atlantic' on a Manchester express composed of the elegant stock, built for the London extension, in dark brown and French grey livery.

Most railway companies have their personalities. Some small ones have seemed to be wholly controlled by one man, sometimes a financier and sometimes an engineer. The Rhymney Railway in South Wales was for many years almost the private property of Cornelius Lundie, who designed the locomotives and controlled everything else until he was about 90 years old. When Arthur Stride neared retirement he arranged to sell 'his' railway, the London, Tilbury and Southend, to the Midland; as a way of 'providing' for it. But although great railways have often been served by great men, the Great Central was really the only great railway that was wholly dependent on a few near-geniuses to keep its head above water for most of its existence after it had assumed that name.

If the above suggests a decrepit concern, with seedy stations, unpunctual trains, uncomfortable carriages and ancient locomotives, then nothing could be further from the truth. The Great Central exuded an air of luxury and prosperity. In fact it had to, if it was to gain any traffic for its long and expensive main line into London, opened in 1899 and operated in direct competition with three long-established and prestigious railways.

Until 1897, this railway had been the Manchester, Sheffield and Lincolnshire, the initials M.S. & L. being popularly interpreted as Muck, Sludge and Lime, or, among the financially knowledgeable, as Money Sunk and Lost. Both of these nicknames were less than fair in earlier days, because though some engineering features, such as the Woodhead tunnel, had made the line expensive to build and therefore short of money, it was a useful and well run railway. Edward Watkin became general manager in 1854, and chairman 10 years later. He was a second 'Railway King', less devious than Hudson, but eventually to prove something of a disaster for the M.S. & L., as for the South Eastern. In the short run, however, he presided over an orderly expansion of his small midlands railway, and it was only his efforts to connect it to London that proved so unfortunate. Attempts to do this over other companies' metals, with real benefits to both parties, foundered on the rock of Watkin's personal ambition, and this ambition could only eventually be satisfied by building the new line into the new London terminus at Marylebone, via the Metropolitan Railway which Watkin himself controlled.

When the London extension was opened Watkin had retired. Such major towns as it passed through already had direct services to London, and the only hope for the newcomer lay in providing very fast, light trains, with excellent coaching stock and plenty of restaurant cars. Goods traffic depended very largely on being able to transfer it to other railways at the London end, and it was the Great Western that proved most helpful: after all, this was a railway that was not in competition.

An undoubted asset from the passenger's point of view was the lovely undulating country traversed by the new line, but the railway undulated as well, for its route was one which earlier lines had avoided for good reasons. Had the goods traffic ever been really heavy on the London extension, this succession of up and down gradients would have presented serious inconvenience to the operation of the standard British loose-coupled freight train. So this was an unnecessary piece of railway, the financial burden of which was to lie heavy upon the Great Central, and later the London and North Eastern. But travelling on it was usually a delight.

Watkin's departure left the stage clear for the entry of the group of exceptionally able men who contrived to make the G.C.R. such an admirable institution. This railway was among the first to make a regular practice of putting the names of directors on its locomotives, and in this case the honour was deserved. One class of locomotive was known as the 'Director' class, but other classes bore such names as well, and the most illustrious were on 'Atlantics' and 4-6-0s. Thus 'Viscount Cross, G.C.B., G.C.S.I.,' a director for 30 years from 1884, was borne upon the curved splasher of a 3-cylinder compound 'Atlantic' or 4-4-2, while Lord Faringdon (previously Alexander Henderson), chairman from 1899 until the grouping, had his name upon the straight splasher of a 4-cylinder simple expansion 4-6-0. A brilliant financier, Faringdon was perhaps chiefly responsible for the company's success against such severe odds, but his general manager, from 1902, Sir Sam Fay (knighted in 1912) was likewise a man of outstanding talent, resource and energy. His name, too, adorned a 4-6-0.

Fay deserves a paragraph to himself. Born in 1856 in Hampshire, he joined the London and South Western Railway as a junior clerk in 1872. Nine years later he

18 Boiler washout for a 'Fish' engine. Great Central goods engines were as handsome as those for passenger service.

launched a 'house journal', the 'South Western Gazette' and soon afterwards published a history of the railway, under the bold title of 'A Royal Road'. Thereafter he rose rapidly, and after a short but successful interlude restoring the fortunes of the Midland and South-Western Junction Railway, he returned to the L.S.W.R. as superintendent of the line in 1899. In 1902 he became general manager of the Great Central, and was knighted in 1912 by King George V on the dockside at Immingham, on the occasion of the opening of this new Great Central port which was largely Fay's creation. After important war work he returned to the railway until the grouping, after which he remained active in locomotive building and overseas railways. He died, aged 96, in 1953 and the writer can still remember the astonishment with which he read a letter to 'The Times' written by Fay shortly before his death, at a time when it seemed to be a voice from the past. His name 'Sir Sam Fay', abrupt and purposeful in sound, adorned one of the most impressive and handsome of all British locomotives (though not one of the most successful) and it also adorned numerous splendid models of that locomotive made by two manufacturers. In this way that name became familiar to a generation of covetous schoolboys who had little idea of the achievements of its owner, but this is usual with the names of the great.

It is to be regretted that no Great Central locomotive ever bore the name of John G. Robinson, the chief mechanical engineer. The magnificent appearance of Great Central trains was due to him, and much excellent and reliable engineering went into them. Technically his locomotives were good but not brilliant, but their appearance was not surpassed anywhere, whether they were small and elegant, or large and imposing. His 'Atlantics' were believed by many to be the loveliest locomotives of all, and were nicknamed 'Jersey Lilies', like the celebrated Edwardian beauty, Lily Langtry. His 2-8-0 freight engines were assembled mainly from the same parts, and were scarcely less handsome. Of this type many

19 Manchester, Sheffield and Lincolnshire Railway 2-4-0, designed by Charles Sacré.

hundreds were built for overseas service during the first World War, to government order, and many of these went overseas again after the second World War, while others were to be found working in the middle and far east and in Australia.

Robinson's coaches were similarly impressive. They looked and were heavy and luxurious, but as the trains were never very long his locomotives worked them with exemplary punctuality. Internally slightly more austere were the large open saloons, the 'Barnums', but these, with their large windows and doors, brass handrails and varnished teak sides, were splendid to look upon, and at least comfortable to ride in. The suburban stock in the London area was also very good, much of it with clerestory roofs, and it was hauled by the most stately of 4-4-2 tank engines, and later by 4-6-2 tanks which looked larger and far more expensive than anything to be seen elsewhere in London working such trains.

All this splendour came with the London extension, and was of a piece with Fay's flair for publicity. The public, not the shareholders, profited—a most democratic arrangement which was not untypical in the world of railways, where many an autocratic management was in fact deeply motivated by a sense of serving the public.

In the humbler beginnings of the railway, the outstanding locomotive engineer was Charles Reboul Sacré, a devoted adherent of the multiframed locomotive structure which had first appeared with Stephenson's 'Planet' on the Liverpool and Manchester Railway in 1830. Flycranks and outside coupling rods even appeared on some 4-4-0s, a piece of antiquarianism which was only equalled in Britain by the Great Western, but Sacré's suspicions of crank axles were justified when one of his 4-4-0s broke one near Penistone. However, the resulting accident was serious, and showed that double framing was not necessarily an effective precaution.

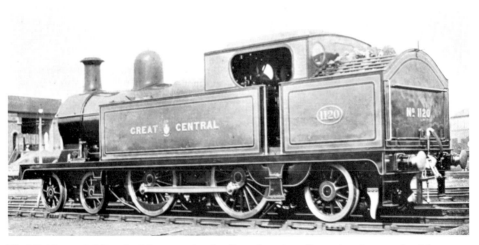

20 A Robinson 4-4-2 tank of the second series. Note the extraordinary cleanliness and polish.

Sacré was a very able engineer, and he left the M.S. & L. with a good and very distinctive locomotive fleet. He was followed by two rather shadowy figures, Thomas Parker and Harry Pollitt. The first of these left much locomotive design to the private builders, Kitson and Company. The results were good and formed the foundation of a new series of designs of 4-4-0, 0-6-0, 0-6-2 tank and 2-4-2 tank, which were perpetuated by Pollitt and improved by Robinson in his early days, though the tank engines were succeeded by larger types. Even so, the older tank engines lasted nearly until the end of steam in Britain, Pollitt locomotives were the first to work the London extension, and among them was a series of 4-2-2s built specially for the light, fast trains planned for the new service. The Pollitt singles were soon displaced, but worked out their lives on the Cheshire Lines joint system, and achieved the distinction of being the only single drivers to receive superheaters.

In the first years of the London Extension, the fast trains consisted of a few eight or twelve-wheeled coaches, of a particularly elegant style. They were painted in 'French grey' above the waistrail, and brown below, had rather low curves to the roofs and numerous narrow, tall windows. The restaurant cars had clerestories. The total effect was light, and matched the Pollitt singles and 4-4-0s admirably. With the growth of traffic, and the advent of Robinson, the coaches were mixed with new ones of rather heavier appearance, their livery became varnished teak, and the locomotives were larger, but still most elegant. However, it was in the last period that Robinson contrived what no other locomotive engineer did so well: he produced engines with really large boilers which yet managed to look neat, perfectly proportioned, and really handsome in a slightly old-fashioned way. The high finish and elaborate livery was set off by the dark teak of the massive 'dreadnought' coaches (a nickname found on the Great Western also) which carried heavy, toothed castings on their ends, to prevent overriding in the case of a collision.

21 2-8-0 freight engine built for the Railway Operating Division of the Royal Engineers, to the G.E.R. 8K design. This type was a war standard and many went overseas in 1914-18.

A fit setting for such trains was provided by Marylebone Station, which had only four platforms, was always clean and quiet, and was well attended by cabs. The large covered forecourt lay between the station and the Great Central Hotel: the large, stately building which is now given over entirely to railway offices and goes under the unevocative name of 222 Marylebone Road. It was all very upper middle class, because even the suburban trains served only expensive and semi-rural towns like Harrow, Rickmansworth and Amersham. Once one reached Nottingham, on the other hand, there were signs of the railway's more workaday purposes. Nottingham Victoria Station itself was jointly owned with the Great Northern, and the more austere outlines of G.N. locomotives, together with the procession of long goods trains which trundled under the high roof, made it plain that one had arrived in the Midlands. It was a spacious but curiously enclosed station, with excellent buildings and good waiting and refreshment rooms, and somehow the trains appeared to behave as if they were aware that they had entered a gracious interior. But it was surrounded by junctions, and there were coal trains everywhere.

The Nottinghamshire coalfield provided a great deal of traffic for the Great Central. Sherwood Forest and the Dukeries, once the location of so many grand houses, were a tangle of intersecting railway tracks, many on embankments, and at night the pleasant landscape (for it was pleasant enough out of sight of the pits) was often made dramatic by the glare from a locomotive firebox cast upwards to the underside of the long trail of steam as one of Robinson's 'Pom Pom' goods engines pounded along on 50 wagons of coal. The Midland and the Great Northern were also to be found hereabouts, but the Central seemed to predominate, especially as it had absorbed in 1907 the Lancashire, Derbyshire and East Coast Railway, an over-ambitiously named line which ran across the Dukeries serving collieries and providing a passenger service between Lincoln and Chesterfield.

Another important Great Central traffic was fish. Grimsby, like the nearby resort of Cleethorpes, was greatly developed by the railway and was the scene of daily fish auctions followed by the departure of trains to London and most of the Midlands, carrying their highly perishable cargo with all possible speed. Robinson's first 4-6-0 design of 1902 was soon dubbed the 'fish' engine, a curious name for a very pretty locomotive, and the later and somewhat larger version of the design was known as the 'Immingham' class—but this name was actually carried on one of the engines. Immingham was the large and modern port opened by the G.C.R. in 1912, and was 4 miles from Grimsby. The railway built a superior type of electric tramway joining the 2 places. From Immingham coal was sent by sea to other ports in Britain and to the continent. It was also the base of the railway's own fleet of steamers carrying general merchandise. Great Central maritime passenger services ran from Grimsby to various northern European ports, and also between Hull and New Holland.

Much of the coal traffic had to be hauled over the Pennines, and through the single-track tunnels at Woodhead. Double-heading of coal trains was almost impossible, because the crew of the second engine would have been asphyxiated. With one engine, conditions were often appalling, especially if the engine started slipping. This tunnel was probably one reason why Robinson's 2-8-0s were so good—they had to be powerful and sure-footed or the enginemen would refuse to work them. Robinson was one of the locomotive engineers who listened to the opinions of the footplatemen.

He also designed some remarkable 0-8-4 tank engines with 3 cylinders, for working the trains up the 'hump' in the large gravity shunting yard at Wath. These had the greatest hauling capacity of any locomotives in Britain at the time, and were also the first 3 cylinder simple expansion engines in regular service in the country. The steep gradients and heavy loads of this corner of the Great Central system led, in L.N.E.R. days, to the building of the unique 6 cylinder 2-8-0 + 0-8-2 Garratt locomotive, which spent virtually its whole life banking trains over the 1 in 40 gradient of the Worsborough incline between Wath and Penistone. This machine had the greatest hauling power of any single unit locomotive in Britain—a record unlikely to be surpassed even with electric traction.

The Great Central was, not surprisingly, a great operator of cross-country services originating and terminating on other systems, so its metals saw many 'foreign' engines, and its own engines visited many 'foreign parts', one 'Atlantic' even reaching Plymouth. Less romantic but equally complex were its connections and running powers in the Liverpool and Manchester areas. The Cheshire Lines, operated by a joint committee of the Great Central, the Great Northern and the Midland, were worked by Great Central locomotives with C.L.C. stock—mostly of G.C. or G.N. design. There was a main line between Liverpool and Manchester: a level road with light, fast trains ideal for the Pollitt 4-2-2s which lasted well into L.N.E.R. days on these services. There were also suburban services, and those in the Liverpool area were thoroughly mixed-up with the Wirral Railway, the Great Western and the Wrexham, Mold and Connah's Quay line. This last was a decrepit affair kept going by faith and great mechanical ingenuity, which the G.C.R. took over in 1904. All these lines were to see Robinson's graceful 4-4-2 tank engines lend style to their operations all through the period of the grouping.

In the south, the entry to Marylebone through the outer London area was over the tracks of the Metropolitan Railway. This was another of Watkin's lines, but with

22 Lining a new cutting on the London extension, in Buckinghamshire.

his departure from the scene difficulties of track occupation began to grow and it soon became necessary for the G.C.R. to find an additional route into its London terminus and into the London railway network. This was achieved with the co-operation of the Great Western. The G.W. and G.C. joint line passed through High Wycombe, and enabled the G.W. to provide better services to Birmingham and its surroundings by a shorter route avoiding Oxford, while the GCR enjoyed a faster route avoiding the suburban services to Aylesbury. The Great Central, then, depended greatly on alliances. Thanks to these, and the quality of its senior officers, it was able to serve the public in a wholly admirable way.

This railway arose from the desire for better communication between the industrial centres of Manchester and Sheffield. Spurred on by the success of the recent Rainhill Trials, the interested businessmen in 1830 sponsored the Sheffield and Manchester Railway to run via Whaley Bridge and Stockport, but because of the difficulties involved in crossing the Pennine ridge by this route, the scheme was abandoned. It was succeeded in 1837 by the Sheffield, Ashton-under-Lyne and Manchester Railway Company formed to build a line from Sheffield across the Pennines via Godley and Penistone and joining the Manchester and Birmingham line at London Road, Manchester. There were still many problems to be faced in implementing this revised scheme, and the engineer Charles Vignoles was soon at odds with the directors over pay and conditions of service, but nevertheless the project went ahead. Vignoles was replaced as engineer by Joseph Locke in 1840 and the line, containing several noteworthy engineering works and absorbing a

23 Anti-telescoping blocks on the ends of the massive 'Dreadnought' coaches, to keep them in line in case of an accident.

considerable portion of the company's resources, was opened throughout in December 1845 on completion of the 3 mile 22 yard tunnel at Woodhead. (At the time of its construction this tunnel was the longest subterranean bore in the country and had taken seven years to build. It was single line until 1852 when the second bore was completed.)

Rapid expansion followed the opening of this one main line and by July 1846 the Sheffield, Ashton-under-Lyne and Manchester Railway had absorbed the Great Grimsby and Sheffield Junction Railway, the Sheffield and Lincolnshire Junction Railway and the Grimsby Dock Company, to become the new Manchester,

Sheffield and Lincolnshire Railway. The M.S. & L. as it was called, was of necessity involved in considerable expenditure on behalf of its component companies in the early part of 1847 to complete their lines to Grimsby, New Holland and Lincoln via Retford, Gainsborough and Barnetby, and this in addition to the recent expense of constructing its own line proved a serious undertaking for the young company from which it never really recovered. In spite of the difficulties however, the network was opened by 1849 and work was well advanced on the docking installations at Grimsby. The Port of Grimsby, largely a creation of the M.S. & L., was one of the main lifelines of the Company, supplying the system with fish to be carried throughout the country and providing an outlet for coal, exported in considerable quantities. By 1852 the main dock was opened and the ancillary equipment installed on land reclaimed from the Humber. By 1863, a fish dock, graving dock and two coal drops had been added and the Deep Sea Fishing Company, sponsored by the M.S. & L., the G.N.R. and the Midland Railway, was bringing over 10,000 tons of fish per annum through the port.

Among the distinguished men who steered the company through the web of railway alliances and counter-alliances, James Allport, the future General Manager of the Midland Railway, was one of the first. He joined the company in 1849, at the invitation of the shareholders worried by the state of the finances and one of his primary tasks was to negotiate with Mark Huish of the London and North Western, at that time forming the 'Euston Square confederacy' against plans of the Great Northern. In order to relieve North Western pressure on its own system, rather than to repress the young Great Northern, the M.S. & L. agreed to become a member of the confederacy and to adopt a policy of non co-operation with the G.N.R. It was to remain in this somewhat uneasy alliance with the L.N.W.R. for the next seven years, but meanwhile within the ranks of the M.S. & L. changes of importance were taking place. Allport left the company for the Midland Railway in 1853 and was succeeded as General Manager by the redoubtable Edward Watkin, second only to George Hudson in the scope of his railway interests. Watkin soon proved himself a strong and determined negotiator and on the collapse of the Euston Square Confederacy in 1857 he was ready with an agreement between his own railway and its more natural ally the Great Northern Railway, enabling the latter to run through trains to Manchester. It was dealings such as this which were subsequently to earn for the M.S. & L. the nickname of 'The Railway Flirt'.

During the next few years, although often in financial straits, the company continued to expand; in 1859 acquiring shares in a group of lines being planned in Cheshire, in 1863 opening the Grimsby–Cleethorpes line and in 1864 leasing the South Yorkshire Railway, so acquiring a line from Barnsley to Barnetby via Doncaster, with branches to Wakefield and Sheffield. The Midland and Great Northern Railways, at various times the two closest allies, were admitted as joint partners to the Cheshire Lines Committee in 1866–7, and with this additional support the Cheshire rail network was eventually extended to link Southport, Altrincham, Chester, Manchester and Liverpool.

Two connections from the Midland Railway, the one near Beighton, the other near Sheffield, were completed in 1870 opening up further trading possibilities with the Midland system and by 1871 the M.S. & L. had built sidings serving 84 collieries and was witnessing a general rise in its merchandise and mineral business receipts. Indeed during the mid 1870s congestion of the lines in South Yorkshire had become a major problem for the company and necessitated widening works around Sheffield, Mexborough, Worsborough and Chapeltown. The acquisition of the new Wigan Junction Railway in 1877, although costing much to complete, gave access to the large coalfields of the Platt Bridge, Bickershaw and West Leigh areas and twelve years later the opening of the remarkable Hawarden swing bridge over the river Dee prepared the way for tapping the coalfields of North Wales. The Wrexham and Ellesmere Railway serving these Welsh mines was opened in 1895 and was controlled by the M.S. & L., as was the Dee, Birkenhead and Liverpool Railway (later the North Wales and Liverpool Company) opened in 1896.

Meanwhile events were taking place which were to change the whole direction of development. An independent line to London, enabling the railway to take its own traffic to the city on its own metals, had been Watkin's dream ever since 1860. In the belief that the road to the south was the road to the prosperity which always seemed to elude the company, Watkin had accepted the invitation to become a member of the board of the Metropolitan Railway in 1872, so gaining a foothold in London, and had begun negotiating for a line to link with the Midland on the one hand and the South Eastern Railway on the other, but nothing had come of the scheme. Time had dragged on with no more positive moves until 1889 when the Beighton to Annesley line was authorised to give the M.S. & L. access to several more collieries in Derbyshire. There was some opposition to the scheme from the Great Northern, fearful of further competition, but it was eventually agreed that Nottingham would be a legitimate objective, using the G.N.R. line from Annesley. The Beighton–Annesley line was opened in 1892 and gave Watkin the opportunity he needed to press for his full London extension.

In the same year 1892, the plans for an M.S. & L. line via Leicester and Nottingham to join the Metropolitan Railway at Quainton Road passed through Parliament. Keen opposition from the Midland and the G.N.R. had been overcome but because of a trade depression and shortage of money Sir Edward Watkin (knighted in 1868) was not able to see the work begin before his retirement as General Manager in May 1894. It was his successor William Pollitt who had the responsibility and privilege of seeing the line opened from Annesley to Quainton Road and from Harrow-on-the-Hill to the newly constructed Marylebone station in 1897. The intervening section (between Quainton Road and Harrow-on-the-Hill) was over Metropolitan metals.

To mark the beginning of this new era in its history the company adopted its new name, the Great Central Railway, and temporarily changed its coaching livery from the previous varnished teak to dark brown with grey upper panels. The first G.C.R. passenger train to run on the new extension left Manchester London Road on 15 March 1899. The joint G.W. and G.C. line was opened in 1905.

The arrival of the G.C.R. in London so many years after the other major companies had become established there meant the beginning of an energetic campaign for traffic on the part of the newcomer. Again the G.C.R. was fortunate in having the services of two outstanding personalities in Sam Fay and W. J. Stuart. One of Fay's first acts was to establish a Publicity Department of which Stuart was made manager. Various types of publicity material were produced including books of matches, note paper, picture postcards, playing cards and of course posters bearing Sam Fay's famous G.C.R. slogan 'Rapid Travel in Luxury'.

In fulfilment of this slogan, passenger services were extended and improved. Pollitt had already introduced dining car expresses from London to Huddersfield, Halifax and Bradford and through trains from Leicester and Nottingham to Blackpool and Fleetwood, but Fay went further and in conjunction with the N.E.R. and the G.W.R. he introduced daily breakfast and luncheon car trains between Newcastle-on-Tyne and Bournemouth. In 1903 came the through corridor express services arranged with the G.E.R. to run from Liverpool and connect with the Manchester express to Sheffield, Lincoln, Yarmouth and Cromer. Suitably luxurious carriages, including 3rd class dining cars finished in oak and non-corridor suburban stock with new type folding arm rests in the 1st class, and mirrors in the 3rd, were introduced for the London service and gained much approbation from the public, being of a generally higher standard than the stock prevailing on other lines at that time. Here was a real reversal of previous trends for the M.S. & L. had usually been one step behind the larger companies in rolling stock design.

In common with most railways of the 1840s, the M.S. & L. had at first provided bare wooden seats and open carriages for its 2nd and 3rd class passengers, but rising standards on neighbouring lines soon exerted a modernising influence on the company. By 1859 cushions were provided in 2nd class main line coaches and 1st class travel was approaching G.N.R. standards while the abolition of 2nd class travel by the Midland Railway in 1874 meant the introduction of umbrella racks, curtains, carpets and other such comforts in the 2nd class coaches of the M.S. & L. The first bogie coaches appeared on the line in 1878 and the first dining car, a joint venture with the Great Northern Railway, was produced in 1884. By 1914 the G.C.R. owned as many as 20 restaurant cars and was one of the few companies to continue several of its restaurant services throughout the war.

Continental connections had long been a feature, beginning in 1852 with the Grimsby to Hamburg and Rotterdam services operated by the North of Europe Steamship Company. In 1864 the railway was allowed to own and operate its own steamers and added Stockholm, St. Petersburg and Kronstadt to its ports of call. There was great competition for this trade from the Lancashire and Yorkshire Railway using the harbour at Goole, but M.S. & L. freight charges and passenger fares were very reasonable and attracted much business. Sailings to Gothenburg began in 1892 and three years later a special service was inaugurated to Antwerp in conjunction with the Cunard shipping company. The arrangement was beneficial to both parties because Cunard found that by discharging its cargo at Liverpool for transportation to Antwerp via Grimsby, it gained four days over its rival, the Red Star Line, which delivered its New York–Antwerp traffic direct.

The crowning achievement of the G.C.R. however, in marine matters, was its creation of the port of Immingham between 1906 and 1912. Increasing pressure on docking facilities at Grimsby had already necessitated further enlargement of the fish docks and improvements in the handling facilities for grain and coal, but nevertheless by the end of the 19th century it had become clear that additional docking areas were necessary. A committee was established to investigate suitable sites and Immingham, a sheltered harbour near Grimsby, was chosen. The project was sanctioned in 1904 and in 1906 work began. It was an ambitious scheme, even more so than the development of Cleethorpes in the 1880s when the company had taken the quiet seaside town and by the addition of sea defences, swimming baths, refreshment rooms and a promenade had transformed it into a holiday resort. It was six years before the building at Immingham was completed but in 1912 the new dock estate, excluding the 45 acres of water area, covered 1000 acres in all.

Between 1910 and 1914 the G.C.R. attained its zenith. These years saw the introduction of through services featuring combined rail and sea trips to the Isle of Man and North Wales, run in conjunction with the Isle of Man Steamship Company and the Liverpool and North Wales Steamship Company. Goods traffic continued to increase, reaching a total of $25\frac{3}{4}$ million tons of minerals and $5\frac{1}{4}$ million tons of merchandise carried by 1910, and widening works were necessary along various stretches of track.

The War years were hard on all railways, and the Great Central was not alone in contributing ships, men and increased services to the war effort. But it made a distinctive contribution in the hundreds of Robinson's freight engines built as a war standard for overseas service, many constructed at the company's works at Gorton, Manchester. After the war, the last and largest Robinson engines and carriages were again beautifully painted and maintained, and a four cylinder 4-6-0 became the War Memorial Engine, bearing the name 'Valour' on large commemorative plates on the splashers.

The London and North Eastern absorbed the Great Central on 1st January 1923. The new administration selected some Great Central locomotive designs for new construction. It had inherited a railway in excellent physical shape, which was little changed for many years, but it had also inherited the financial problems. Nothing daunted, the new company adopted as its own the brave motto of the Great Central: 'Forward'. The adoption of 'Forward' was prophetic, for not only did the L.N.E.R. prove outstandingly progressive, but it was always, like the Great Central, short of money. And like the Great Central it owed its splendid achievements to a few near-geniuses cast in the mould of Lord Faringdon, and Sir Sam Fay.

Major routes of the Lancashire and Yorkshire Railway

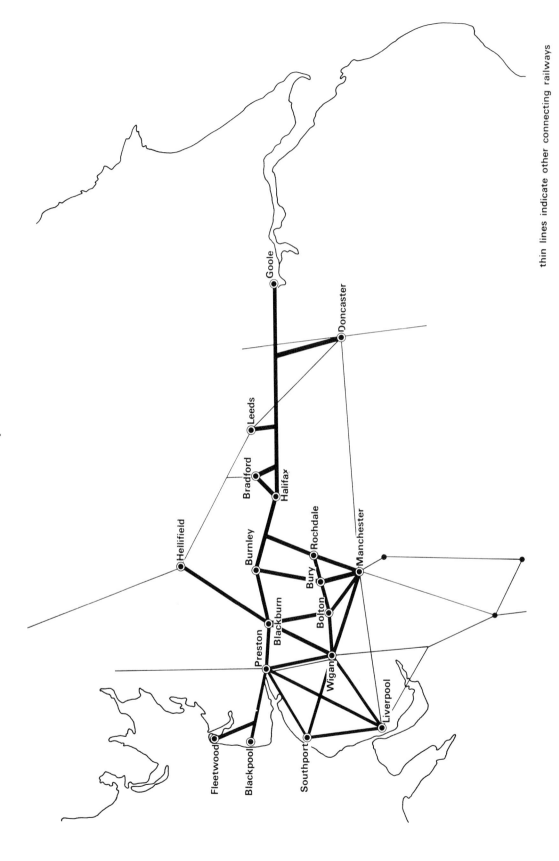

thin lines indicate other connecting railways

The Lancashire and Yorkshire Railway

24 L.Y.R. Aspinall 'Atlantic' at speed, an image of grace and pace.

If you took a pregrouping map of the railways of England, perhaps with the different companies' tracks marked in different colours, the area stretching from north Cheshire and Lancashire on the West across to the coastline of Yorkshire with a little of Lincolnshire, on the East, would seem to present a picture of unprofitable competition: a dense tangle of interwoven lines joining many of the same places by routes which hardly differed from one another. Yet there was a time when most of these lines were profitable. There was much traffic, and the lines had grown in response to real local needs.

Looking more closely at the map, you would see many lines belonging to the

Lancashire & Yorkshire Railway.

THE BUSINESS LINE.

West to East Coast Express.

To anyone who has a knowledge of English geography the words Lancashire and Yorkshire at once convey suggestions of great activity and commercial development. These counties are the chief homes of our great manufacturing and mineral industries, and the fact that the Lancashire & Yorkshire Railway serves these busy hives of industry gives emphasis to the well deserved title, " The Business Line," by which the Lancashire & Yorkshire Railway is so well known.

The system connects the West and East Coasts of England, and crosses more or less at right angles all the North and South Lines, affording an excellent means of communication with other parts of the Kingdom. A feature of the progressive policy of the Lancashire & Yorkshire Railway is the inauguration of numerous through and direct services to various parts of the country. The following list includes some of the most important and popular services :—Colne, Burnley, Accrington, Blackburn, Bolton, Manchester (Victoria) and London (Euston) ; Bradford (Exchange), Halifax, Huddersfield, &c., and Sheffield, London (St. Pancras), Bristol, Bath and South and West of England via Thornhill and Midland Line ; Manchester (Victoria), Liverpool (Exchange) and Glasgow and Edinburgh via West Coast and Midland routes respectively ; Liverpool (Exchange), Manchester (Victoria), York and Newcastle (dining cars) ; Liverpool (Exchange), Manchester (Victoria) and Hull ; Liverpool (Exchange), Manchester (Victoria) and the Lake District ; Liverpool (Exchange), Manchester (Victoria) and Doncaster in connection with the Continental Boat Train via Harwich ; express services between Lancashire and Yorkshire (West Riding) towns and Bournemouth (West), Southampton and Portsmouth.

Two outstanding progressive features in matters of transport are : (1) The electrification of important sections of the system in the Liverpool and Southport districts, also between Bury and Holcombe Brook, the Company now having a total of 87 miles of single track electrified. (2) From joint ownership with another Company of a few passenger steamers the Lancashire & Yorkshire Railway has become the largest owner amongst British Railways of passenger and cargo steamships.

The Steamship Services are as follows :—Goole to Antwerp, Amsterdam, Bruges, Copenhagen, Delfziel Dunkirk, Ghent, Hamburg and Rotterdam ; Liverpool and Drogheda ; Fleetwood and Belfast (L. & Y. and L. & N. W. Railways).

For further particulars of Passenger Services, Guide Books, &c., apply to Mr. A. WATSON, Superintendent of the Line, Manchester ; and to Mr. H. MARRIOTT, Chief Goods Manager, Manchester, for information respecting Goods Traffic.

Hunt's Bank,
Manchester.

JOHN A. F. ASPINALL,
General Manager.

25 L.Y.R. publicity, 1914, with a Hughes 4-6-0 as first built great trunk railways. The London and North Western was there, of course, and the Midland. The Great Northern, the Great Central and the North Eastern all sent lines out of the tangle into the rest of England and beyond. Even the Great Western virtually reached Liverpool by running to Birkenhead. But there were little railways too, like the Wrexham, Mold and Connah's Quay, and joint railways owned by great companies, like the Cheshire Lines, which offered one of the three express routes between Liverpool and Manchester. Unlike any of these, and tightly knitted into the pattern, was the Lancashire and Yorkshire Railway.

The L.Y.R. was the only big railway that ran mainly crosswise over the map of England, in the North. Its distances were not as great as those of the North to South railways, but its traffic was dense and its routes were hard. Its passenger trains carried few southerners and its preoccupation was indicated by its self chosen soubriquet 'the business line'.

It is hard to paint a word picture of the character of this railway, yet anyone who used the L.M.S. between the wars in this part of the country was keenly aware that this was a long way from Euston, St. Pancras or Carlisle. It was mostly raining on the old L.Y.R. tracks, and everything that could be seemed to be made of large blocks of dark stone. 0-6-0 goods locomotives of great effectiveness and singularly ugly outline led long rakes of loose coupled goods wagons round endless curves and up and down stone switchbacks. In a place like Wigan it seemed as if the train one had seen at one bridge immediately turned back to reappear at the next, going the other way. But the peculiar ugliness of the large 0-6-0 locomotives working so much of this unglamorous traffic came from the fitting of superheaters, and one of these machines was the very first British loco-motive to be equipped with this important improvement in its definitive form.

General goods traffic, then, seemed to predominate, but it was closely followed by mineral traffic, in even longer trains and mostly handled by 0-8-0 locomotives which were elongated versions of the other ones, but somehow more elegant (though there were a few of the type which were much heftier in appearance and looked top heavy). Passenger trains in pregrouping days were painted in two shades of brown: a sort of tawny buff around the windows and dark brown beneath. The locomotives were black, with red and white lines, and those tender engines to be found on passenger trains were mostly possessed of a remarkable, lean elegance. This effect was enhanced by the possession of four coupled wheels with a diameter no less than 7 ft. 3 in. (2.21 m.) This switchback of a railway was in fact the only one to possess a large fleet of locomotives with coupled wheels as large as this.

The impression of a switchback railway, though strong enough, really was rather misleading. The Manchester and Leeds Railway, from which the L.Y.R. was descended, had been laid out early and opened between Manchester and Normanton in 1840. Having first choice of route across the hilly centre of England, it followed river valleys as far as possible, and its Summit tunnel was less formidable an undertaking than those of the other three railways which came later. There were eventually nearly a hundred tunnels on the whole system, and a similar number of viaducts, but this was symptomatic of the engineers' concern to keep

26 A Hawkshaw 2-4-0 of the early years.

gradients down. All the same, there were some spectacular climbs round Wigan, Burnley and elsewhere, and out of Manchester up to Miles Platting (originally rope worked), while an enduring memory is of one of the 2-4-2 tank engines trailing ten coaches and thumping its way doggedly up the bank to Baxenden.

Out of a total mileage of 585, only 25 miles of track were level, and civil engineering works were numerous, if not specially elaborate. Over the years many of the viaducts had to be strengthened or replaced by earthworks, and also over the years the districts served by the railway became more built up and densely populated, till there was little rural scenery left. This was not a railway fitting naturally in the landscape, a gracious and sometimes grand addition. It was mostly a railway as a man-made feature in man-made scenery: impressive at times, curiously picturesque in some places, but seldom beautiful.

In the early days, though the railway was more rural, it was decidely ramshackle and had a reputation for discomfort and unreliability quite as bad as that later attributed to the London, Chatham and Dover. Excellent contemporary models of the Manchester and Leeds coaches, relettered L.Y.R., have survived, and these exceedingly short vehicles, on four wheels, offered two small wooden boxes for first class passengers, and benches in the open for second, while the thirds had no seats, their only amenity being holes in the floors to let the rain out in wet weather; to ensure that the passengers would not actually drown in company property, though they might catch their death of cold or be choked with the fumes of half burnt coke in all those tunnels (it is only fair to add that other railways had such vehicles as well). The locomotives were little 16 tonners, of a type devised by Sir John Hawkshaw, with outside cylinders overhanging at the front end, the driving axle just before the firebox and a coupled axle behind it, the arrangement being 2-4-0 in the Whyte notation. This layout became the most popular for passenger locomotives in Germany until the 1890s, but was never common in Britain, where inside cylinders were preferred.

In 1876, the railway acquired the services of Barton Wright as engineer, and for

27 Barton Wright 0-6-2 tank locomotive, with arc-roofed coaches.

ten years he struggled to improve matters, until he escaped to something better in India. Wright was a good engineer, hardly remembered now, and in his day bogie coaches first appeared on the line—moreover, they were twelve wheelers, in a bold attempt to provide a smooth ride over poor track. His locomotives introduced that note of elegance which was so successfully sounded by his successors, and included examples of two characteristic British types, the 4-4-0 and the 0-6-0. He was also the one who introduced the L.Y.R. practice of using tank engines on express trains, though in his day 'express' signified distance covered and importance of the route rather than speed. There was a long series of Barton Wright 0-4-4 tanks, and these in their early days worked between Manchester and Leeds. Perhaps Wright's greatest claim to be remembered lies in his introduction of the 0-6-2 tank type, in 1879. This wheel arrangement was eventually used by almost all British railway companies, on a wide range of duties, and it would be difficult to imagine the South Wales coal railways functioning efficiently without it, so it would certainly have been introduced in due course by someone else if Wright had not had the idea first, but this does not detract from the credit he deserves for his perceptiveness. The L.Y.R. did not often construct locomotives at either of its works at Miles Platting or Bury, so the detail design of his engines was largely carried out by Kitson and Co., of Leeds.

Wright's successor was J. A. F. Aspinall, later knighted, a very able engineer. Crewe trained and with experience as locomotive engineer of the Great Southern and Western Railway of Ireland, Aspinall is one of the most remarkable figures of Britain's railway heyday. His thirteen years as mechanical engineer saw such improvement in every department that in 1899 he was appointed general manager of the railway—the only example in this country of such a translation. He subsequently transformed the whole system into one of such efficiency and prestige that when the L.M.S. was formed L.Y.R. officers filled many key positions in the new administration.

Aspinall's first and perhaps most important work as engineer was the creation of the new railway works at Horwich, from which the first newly constructed

28 Aspinall 4-4-0 after rebuilding with superheater, piston valves and raised boiler.

locomotive emerged early in 1889. This was the first of the famous L.Y.R. 2-4-2 tanks, a type of which no less than 330 were built, the last in 1911. Horwich was in its day a thorqughly up to date and scientifically oriented factory, and in these respects, if not in size, was the best inherited by the L.M.S. at the grouping. Only a man of Aspinall's energy, vision, and sheer persuasiveness could have caused the still rather seedy L.Y.R. to build so admirable a works, and these same qualities later transformed the management of the railway in almost all respects: most obviously in the frequency, speed and comfort of the trains.

The Aspinall locomotives were at first conventional for their period, except in the adoption of the very large diameter of the coupled wheels of his 4-4-0s. But when the challenge of heavier and more comfortable rolling stock arose on all British railways at the end of the nineteenth century, Aspinall produced a remarkable type of express locomotive quite unlike anything else in this country before or since. He was a close friend of H. A. Ivatt of the Great Northern, who had just produced the first British 'Atlantics' or 4-4-2 type. Ivatt's large machine tactfully concealed its size and was immediately acceptable to the engine crews because it could be seen to be an improved version of the principal previous express type, the Stirling eight-foot single driver, to which it presented many similarities such as the outside cylinders and deep narrow gate. Aspinall copied Ivatt—not in the design but in the philosophy—and produced an inside cylindered 4-4-2, with the same very large coupled wheels as his 4-4-0s, with generally similar mechanism and with again a deep narrow grate. This engine, however, did not conceal its size. With those coupled wheels the boiler had to be pitched high and made the engine look enormous. The engines were immediately christened 'High Flyers'.

The 40 Aspinall 'Atlantics' were, in practice if not in theory, the best L.Y.R. express engines until some time after 1918, so their heyday coincided with the best years of the company. They worked the fast 40 minute expresses between Liverpool and Manchester (of which the L.Y.R. ran almost as many as the other two railways put together) and residential trains of corridor coaches for wealthy commuters from places like Blackpool and Lytham. They ran longer distance expresses between Liverpool, Manchester, Leeds and York, and boat trains for Belfast to Fleetwood, or for Rotterdam to Hull. A few of them received a form of low temperature superheat involving an extra steam drum in the smokebox, with firetubes in it, but they never received the normal type of superheater as later fitted to the 4-4-0s. Had they done so, there can be little doubt that one of them would have established a speed record which could have been fully authenticated. As it was, there were several claims of their reaching 100 miles per hour which cannot be regarded as impossible, and one claim of 117, which unfortunately can.

In 1900, the year after the appearance of the first 'Atlantic', Aspinall applied the big engine policy to freight working, with his first 0-8-0, this time just anticipating Ivatt. These inside cylinder engines were later built with 8 wheeled tenders, the result being one of the neatest-looking of all heavy freight machines. A still later batch appeared as four cylinder compounds. Eventually, there were 295 L.Y.R. 0-8-0s, the later versions built by Hughes with very large boilers and side window cabs, and there were five examples of an 0-8-2 tank version. All of these were extremely successful.

At this time, new construction of 0-6-0 and 0-8-0 engines resulted in a large surplus of very good Barton Wright 0-6-0s, which were rather small for the traffic of this boom period. The railway was also short of good shunting engines, because, apart from Aspinall's own 0-4-0 dock tanks, most were very old and of many different types designed by their commercial builders. Some were real historic relics, but in those days this did nothing to ensure their preservation. Aspinall resolved the problems by converting no fewer than 230 of Wright's 0-6-0s into saddle tanks—a very simple and cheap operation which produced a large fleet of highly effective engines, well liked by their crews. Many of these shunters lasted well into the 1950s and a few to 1960, one being then 82 years old. An engine which escaped this conversion survived to be preserved in its original form, and to star in the film 'The Railway Children'.

The 0-8-0 design actually took the rails after H. A. Hoy had replaced Aspinall on the latter's elevation to the general managership. Hoy tried to apply the big engine policy to the passenger tank locomotive stock, by building a very large inside cylinder 2-6-2 tank, but these engines were soon transferred to goods work. Otherwise, he developed his predecessor's designs and made some experiments with compounding, corrugated steel fireboxes and other devices. The major changes were made after George Hughes succeeded Hoy in 1904, and of these the first was the adoption of modern superheating.

To the enthusiast of the time Hughes may have seemed to be something of a vandal, because he destroyed the elegance of the Aspinall designs. Reference has already been made to the ugliness of the superheated 0-6-0s, and to the enormously fat boilers which made many of the 0-8-0s look top heavy. The 4-4-0s did not go unscathed either. But a few of these, which received Walschaerts valve gear in place of the original Joy gear, Belpaire instead of round-topped fireboxes, and superheaters requiring smokeboxes extended well forward, complete with eagerly advanced chimney—these few were in fact astonishingly improved in their performance. They were the equal of the 'Atlantics' and one could wish that the 'Atlantics' had received similar treatment. Hughes also developed the 2-4-2 tank. These engines had two-way water scoops to enable them to pick up water from track troughs when running in either direction, and later batches had lengthened bunkers to take more coal. Superheating and Belpaire fireboxes came to the tanks too, and the last ones had $20\frac{1}{2}''$ cylinders, making them by far the most powerful examples of this wheel arrangement anywhere. The recorded performances of these engines show them to have been the equals of much larger machines on other lines. Among four coupled passenger tanks only the largest Brighton engines regularly exceeded their power output, and many 2-6-2 and 4-6-2 tank types were not superior. The quality of the 2-4-2 tank performance must certainly have owed something to the fact that they carried little surplus weight and had the minimum number of wheels.

The superheated tanks were put onto shorter distance express work, and though the fastest trains were reserved for Atlantics and 4-4-0s, they frequently worked at start-to-stop average speeds of over 50 m.p.h. This came to an end after a number of accidents which suggested that the engines had too few wheels for their weight, to be allowed to run so fast. In one case a broken coupled axle spring was the cause, in another the permanent way had been pushed inches sideways on quite a gentle curve taken at high speed. The result was that they were put on slower but often heavier trains. They did a phenomenal amount of work, in spite of which some of them lasted for sixty years. The first of them is preserved, in the National Railway Museum at York, fittingly, because this type, more than any other and for longer, epitomised the old L.Y.R. system, even in L.M.S. days.

In June 1908 the new brutalism of Hughes' regime was expressed in a new and huge express engine. It was perhaps not quite as ugly as it seems in retrospect, because one's view is coloured by the knowledge of what those engines looked like after their complete transformation from 1920 onwards. In their later state they were very nice looking, but did not for long carry the characteristic fully spelt out legend 'LANCASHIRE & YORKSHIRE' on their tender sides.

Hughes' four-cylinder 4-6-0 was very powerful but very unsatisfactory in its original form. Two sets of Joy valve gear, placed inside, worked all four valves and gave endless mechanical trouble as well as unreliable valve timing. The steam and exhaust connections in the smokebox were difficult to keep tight because of the straining of the structure when running. The common fault of early British 4-6-0s was also present: the rear of the fire went dead because the rear of the ashpan choked up, the rise of the ashpan bottom over the high rear axle being the cause of the trouble. So these twenty engines spent half their time being repaired, and only the conditions of wartime prevented their being rebuilt earlier.

Five were scrapped unrebuilt. The other fifteen were eventually joined by fifty

29 A 'fireproof' open brake third carriage.

five new ones, making seventy examples of the revised Hughes 4-6-0. The front had been completely redesigned and there were now two sets of Walschaerts gear outside, driving four large, long travel, piston valves. The rear end was lengthened and provided with a large and comfortable cab, and there was, of course, a superheater.

They had 6 ft. 3 in. driving wheels—a size chosen to make them suitable for express goods work if necessary. In the early days of the L.M.S. this made them preferred for the L.N.W.R. main line to Scotland between Crewe and Carlisle where the main gradients occurred. And it is as L.M.S. engines that they are best remembered: at first in red, seen in many publicity pictures, and later in black and looking rather sad, pottering about their old haunts on trains of small importance and usually very dirty. Some lasted through the last war.

George Hughes was the first Chief Mechanical Engineer of the L.M.S. but retired in a year or two, after which the locomotive affairs of that railway were notably ill-conducted, chiefly because the engineering side was given no money and no freedom worth speaking of. This was a great folly, because a railway is after all entirely dependent on engineering.

It resulted in no proper further development of the Hughes 4-6-0s. George Hughes built ten of his 4-6-0s as 4-6-4 tanks, in 1924, for the L.M.S., and his final design, which might claim to be the last of the L.Y.R. line, was the 'Horwich' 2-6-0, the numerous class of general purpose locomotive which, with very large piston valves and long valve travel were certainly the most modern machines produced in the early days of the L.M.S.

The Lancashire and Yorkshire was a pioneer of electrification, using multiple unit trains. The first trials of electric trains on the Liverpool-Southport line took place late in 1903, and the full service began in October of the following year, the power supply being generated in the railway's own power station at Formby. Like the North Eastern Railway electric stock of the same period, the carriages had a decidedly American look, with end doors, large windows, open saloon interiors and clerestories. The multiple unit train was, of course, an American invention, and such trains were often referred to as Sprague trains after their inventor, in their early days. Electric working between Manchester and Bury began in 1916, following an experimental opening three years earlier of the Branch from Bury to Holcombe Brook, using overhead current collection at 3000 volts. This first part was soon converted to third rail and 1200 volts. Again, the power station was railway owned.

The rolling stock on these electrified lines was constructed mainly (and later wholly) of metal, with all-steel underframes and some use of aluminium for panelling. Similar standards were applied in Hughes' 'fireproof' express stock of 1914, which was inspired by the disastrous fire in gaslit stock on the Midland railway in the Ais Gill disaster. The L.Y.R. was understandably anxious to preserve the public confidence in gas lighting, to which it was still heavily committed. The older bogie stock of the L.Y.R. was characterised by the sharp edge of the roof, which was curved in a circular arc instead of the more usual semi-ellipse. The corridor stock was distinctive, including saloons with recessed end doors, some of which had worked in exclusive 'Club' trains for wealthy long distance commuters. There was also a unique ten-wheeled kitchen car built for the first corridor dining-car train which started running between Fleetwood and Leeds in 1901. When L.M.S. livery covered that of all the L.M.S. pre-grouping constituents there was still no difficulty in picking out the ex L.Y.R. stock.

Like most railways, the Lancashire and Yorkshire went in for rail motors in the first years of this century. These curious combinations of very small locomotives and special carriages, arranged to be driven from either end, lasted better on the L.Y.R. than on most other systems, and quite a number of the eighteen built were still around in the 1930s, providing brisk but uncomfortable travel on little used routes. The earlier ones were built to a design from the Taff Vale Railway, but a much more effective type was designed by Hughes for later construction. Even smaller (by several orders of magnitude) were the locomotives of that well-known L.Y.R. institution, the 18" gauge works railway at Horwich. This was an Aspinall brain child and provided an efficient way of carrying raw materials and small parts in and out of the workshops. It was a delightfully toylike little railway, the locomotives bearing the names Wren, Dot, Robin, Wasp, Fly, Mouse, Midget and Bee. The first of these is happily preserved in the National Railway Museum at York.

Another essay in mechanical handling was the overhead railway in Manchester Victoria Station. Small electric locomotives ran high up on a track suspended from the roof. Beneath them, their drivers rode with legs horizontal above a large wicker skip, which could be lowered to platform level for loading and unloading, before taking to the air for its journey around the station.

The Grand National at Aintree was a major event in the L.Y.R. calendar. Specially marshalled electric trains brought the crowds from Liverpool, and numerous steam trains arrived from other parts of the railway, and from other railways as well. The emptying and disposal of these trains, and their subsequent refilling and despatch in the evening, were done with remarkable speed. This was perhaps only to be expected of the railway that served Blackpool, where the same sort of problem presented itself on many days of the year. Race trains, wakes weeks, and bank holidays provided some of the most memorable images of most railways. The sight of ten trains, sometimes with ten identical locomotives, all polished up and ready to go, would often make the thousands packed on the platforms raise mighty cheers of anticipation and admiration. On such days every locomotive was noble, and every engine crew heroic—it was all part of the pageant of steam, part of a world now vanished and almost unimaginable, and its place in the bank holiday ritual is now taken by the five-mile traffic jam.

Like its larger neighbours the N.E.R. and the L.N.W.R., the L.Y.R. was formed by the fusion of several smaller concerns. It dated from July 1847 when the enterprising Manchester and Leeds company, having expanded far beyond its original confines, changed its name to the Lancashire and Yorkshire Railway. The Manchester and Leeds, opened in 1840 with a line stretching not to Leeds but from Manchester via Hebden Bridge to Normanton, had gained control over no less than eight independent companies just before changing its name, to gain connections with the east and west coast ports and with the major towns of the region. First had come the Bolton and Preston line, a part of the North Union Railway, leased jointly by the Manchester and Leeds and Grand Junction Railways in January 1846. Then in July, came two more lines: the Liverpool and Bury, authorised in 1844, and the Huddersfield and Sheffield of 1845. They were followed in August by the Manchester and Bolton opened in 1831 (the oldest section of the L.Y.R.) and in December by the West Riding Union Railway, just three months after its incorporation. The Preston and Wyre, with its branches to Lytham and Blackpool was to have joined the M. & L.R. in August 1846 but in fact was vested jointly in the L.Y.R. and the L.N.W.R. in 1849. The last two acquisitions by the Manchester and Leeds (the Wakefield, Pontefract and Goole and the Ashton, Stalybridge and Liverpool Junction Railways) came in the Act of 1847 by which the company changed its name. In 1847, the future looked hopeful, with the possibility of developing the Lancashire coastal resorts of Blackpool, Lytham and Southport, and with the promise of lucrative traffic from the Lancashire cotton mills, the Yorkshire woollen mills and the coal mines. The very nature of the region suggested heavy traffic patterns and would have augured well had it not been for managerial deficiencies in the 1860s and 1870s which nearly proved disastrous for the company. In developing its track network to take advantage of opportunities, and in blocking certain rival schemes while at the same time attempting to encourage shareholders by high dividends, the company was soon to find itself with decrepit rolling stock, congested lines, unreliable services and an unfortunate reputation for being the worst-run line in the country.

In 1847 however, all this lay ahead and the immediate task for the L.Y.R. was to complete those lines still under construction when amalgamated with the M. & L.R. The Liverpool and Bury, which, with the Heywood extension, gave the L.Y.R. a competing route with the L.N.W.R. from Liverpool to Manchester, was opened throughout in 1848 and contained some noteworthy engineering works, including a 700 ft. long viaduct over the River Croal and the canal. This had six 73 ft. lattice girder spans on stone piers and was among the earliest of the kind in England. Also completed in 1848 was the Wakefield, Pontefract and Goole line connecting the L.Y.R. with Continental steamer services inaugurated the following year. The Huddersfield and Sheffield Junction was completed to Penistone in 1850, to join the M.S. & L., while the West Riding Union was opened from Low Moor to Bradford also in 1850, giving the L.Y.R. access to the well known iron works, but costs had so depleted L.Y.R. funds that plans for the Leeds extension were dropped. New lines were built from Rochdale to Bacup between 1861 and 1870 and from Blackburn via Chorley to Wigan in 1864-9 to counter rival schemes from the M.S. & L. and the L.N.W.R. respectively. Further expansion of the track network was centred in Lancashire when in 1855 L.Y.R. after long preliminary negotiations, bought the Liverpool, Crosby and Southport Railway, and the Manchester and Southport line, which it had helped to build from Southport to Wigan. These acquisitions, soon to prove among the most profitable L.Y.R. passenger routes, resulted in renewed conflict with the East Lancashire Railway, whose lines ran from Clifton Junction to Accrington, Burnley and Colne, and from Accrington via Ormskirk to Preston and Liverpool. This conflict ended in the amalgamation of the two concerns in 1858/9. The Blackburn Railway also had been virtually compelled to join the L.Y.R. in 1858 to ensure its own survival. With its line from Bolton to Chatburn it gave the L.Y.R. the basis for its most northerly station at Hellifield, the Chatburn to Hellifield extension being built between 1871 and 1879 to connect with the Midland Railway. The track network was completed when the L.Y.R. absorbed the West Lancashire and the Liverpool, Southport and Preston Railways in 1897 and gained shares in the South Yorkshire Railway opened from Dinnington to Kirk Sandall in 1909, and the Axholme Joint Railway opened from Marshland to Haxey in 1904. The Dearne Valley Railway, with a line from Brierley just outside Wakefield to the G.N.R. and G.E.R. joint line south of Doncaster, was worked by the L.Y.R. from its opening in 1908 but remained an independent company until 1923.

By 1871, the year the L.Y.R. centralised its administration in Manchester, it was already acquiring a reputation for unreliability and discomfort. This was partly due to mismanagement of resources in the early years and partly due to the nature of the track network itself. It was undoubtedly a difficult road to work with several steep gradients and numerous stations and branch lines, the longest non-stop run being only 48 miles. Consequently even by contemporary standards L.Y.R. express trains were slow. The situation was only aggravated as the volume of traffic on the L.Y.R. increased and by 1872 it was not unusual for passengers to be delayed for up to an hour because goods trains were blocking the lines. Furthermore the L.Y.R. carriages were not always of the best and the old 2-2-2 and 2-4-0 locomotives were proving unequal to their task.

It took a good twenty years for the L.Y.R. to rectify all the deficiencies but by the 1890s significant progress had been made. The men responsible for the transformation were William Barton Wright, locomotive superintendent from 1875 to 1885, John Pearson and George Armytage, chairmen of the company from 1883-7 and 1887 to 1918 respectively and John Aspinall.

Great improvements were necessary in the track network, and accordingly widening works were begun on the Manchester and Bolton line around Salford, on the Liverpool and Bury line through Hindley and Kirkdale, on the Manchester and Normanton line around Brighouse, Wakefield and Rochdale and on the Manchester North Docks Branch line. To ease congestion around Liverpool, the Aintree marshalling yard and the sidings at Fazakerly were built in 1881, the Southport

30 Ambitious if disloyal L.Y.R. advertising.

line was widened around Bootle and a loop line provided at Sandhills. A new passenger station, Liverpool Exchange, was opened in 1888 along with a 150 bedroomed hotel, and in 1889 the new Pendleton to Hindley line was completed cutting $3\frac{1}{2}$ miles off the journey from Manchester to Liverpool. The new Manchester Victoria station, an enlargement of the 1844 original, was opened in 1884 and in 1898 was fitted with its overhead parcel and luggage railway. The modern, well equipped locomotive works, covering 116 acres, was built at Horwich in 1886. The carriage and wagon department had also been removed from Miles Platting in 1877 and was re-established at Newton Heath.

The local papers, once loud in their condemnation of the company, by 1884 were reporting on the enterprise displayed and the regard shown for passengers in the operation of the daily train services. Excursions, always popular on the L.Y.R. line, especially at Whitsuntide, had been extended in scope. While still running outings to Blackpool and Southport, the company now offered additional cheap trips to Bolton Abbey, Ilkley, Scarborough and the Lake District. Working closely with the five major north-south railways crossing its lines, the G.N.R., the N.E.R. the L.N.W.R., the G.C.R. and the Midland Railway, the Lancashire and Yorkshire introduced new joint or through services in 1903 between Manchester and Scarborough, in 1904 between Manchester and Windermere, in 1905 between Bradford, Halifax and North Wales, in 1908 between Liverpool and Newcastle, in 1909 between

Bradford and Marylebone and in 1911 between Southport, Birmingham and Bournemouth. To attract more passengers to the line a publicity department was established in 1906 and through it the L.Y.R. did much to popularise the beauty spots of the Pennines, offering as a special attraction combined tours involving from four to twenty miles of walking. Of similar publicity value was the Golf Link Guide published in 1909 in which the company gave full details of the golf courses reached by its railway network. For the benefit of Manchester business men willing to pay first class fare, a new type of commuter train, the club train for members only, was introduced in 1895 between Blackpool and Manchester. They were luxuriously appointed, consisting of specially built carriages with open saloons, a running buffet and lounge chairs, and were timed to leave Blackpool at 7.18 and 8.20 each morning, returning from Manchester at 5.10 and 5.15 each afternoon. Further commuter traffic to and from Manchester was encouraged in 1916 when the Manchester-Bury line was electrified. With journey times reduced to 24 minutes a publicity campaign was launched to inform the public of the advantages of living in the healthy Manchester suburbs. Rather surprisingly perhaps, the L.Y.R. was not a line which encouraged its third class passengers and it was not until 1878 that the company had allowed them on all its trains, and not until 1912 that it finally abolished the second class fare.

Alongside the developing passenger services, the volume of goods traffic handled annually by the L.Y.R. was mounting steadily to its 1910 total of 7 million tons of merchandise and 18 million tons of minerals carried, much of which passed through the ports of Liverpool, Fleetwood and Goole. Resources were concentrated on developing the docking facilities of Fleetwood and Goole with the building of the fish dock at Fleetwood in 1906-9 and the Stanhope, South and West Docks at Goole in 1891 and 1912. High capacity wagons of 20 and 30 tons were produced by the company in 1901/2 and central traffic control, essential on such a complex and crowded system, was introduced for goods trains in 1913. Numerous ships, sailing from Goole, connected with the L.Y.R. services and carried the manufactures and minerals of Lancashire and Yorkshire to Rotterdam, Antwerp, Bruges and other Continental ports. From Fleetwood in Lancashire, in conjunction with the L.N.W.R., the company ran regular steamer services to Belfast, and in 1902, on buying the ships of the Drogheda Steam Packet Co., began operating the service from Liverpool to Drogheda. By 1910 the L.Y.R. had the distinction of owning more steamers than any other British railway company. It was also one of the first companies to install electropneumatic signalling, which it fitted at Bolton in 1904.

On the 1 January 1922, the independent existence of the L.Y.R. came to an end when the company was absorbed by the L.N.W.R. The amalgamation was not unexpected as the two railways had worked closely together for many years and had proposed that such a step be taken as early as 1872. For the L.Y.R. it did not mean oblivion, for the general manager, the secretary and chief mechanical engineer retained their posts in the joint company, and on the formation of the L.M.S. continued in positions of responsibility.

31 Sir John Aspinall.

Major routes of the South Eastern and Chatham Railway

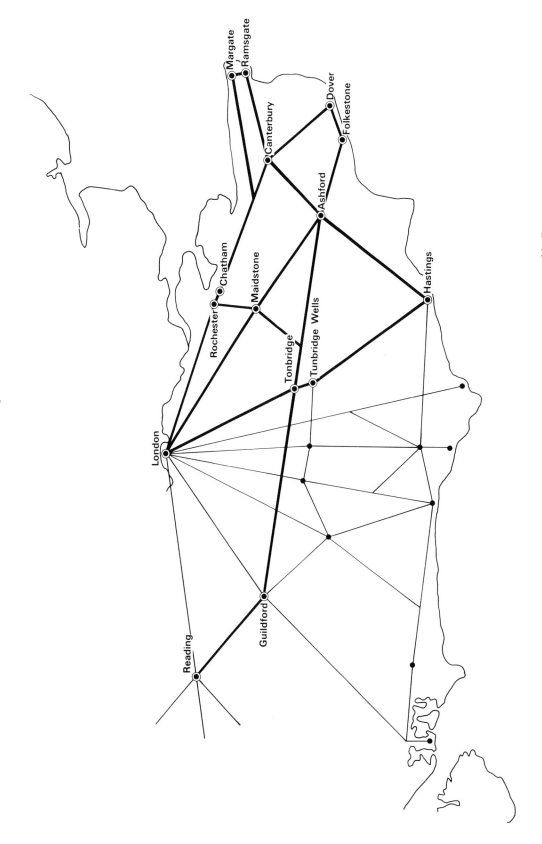

thin lines indicate other connecting railways

The South Eastern and Chatham Railway

32 A Wainwright class D 4-4-0, beflagged in honour of the 'Entente Cordiale' of Edward VII's reign. This locomotive is now in the National Railway Museum.

This railway was in fact two old rivals, operated by a joint managing committee from 1899. To the traveller, these rivals were very similar in character by all accounts, and their amalgamation produced less change than might have been hoped for, because Parliamentary agreement was subject to conditions which excluded that rationalisation of services from which economies and prosperity would perhaps have resulted. However, a publicity-conscious managing committee, ably assisted by an artistically inclined locomotive and carriage designer, certainly raised the esteem in which the railway was held by the continental traveller and the wealthier commuter from the south east coast.

The South Eastern Railway, the older partner, was magnificently engineered by Sir William Cubitt,, and included two remarkable features: 48 miles of virtually straight and level track from Redhill to Ashford, and the line along the sea from Folkestone to Dover which pierces the high chalk cliffs in four tunnels. Between the tunnels the line runs some way above high water mark, but in rough weather spray reaches the trains and this can still be a dramatic piece of railway. A number of slips and blockages have occurred here, the most serious being in December 1915, which actually led to the abandonment of the route for the duration of the war. On that occasion no lives were lost, but a locomotive and four coaches had to

33 Building Cannon St. Station and bridge, 1865.

be winched back from the brink of the crumbling chalk. Perhaps the most spectacular part of the construction was the use of some 8 tons of gunpowder to blast away the face of Round Down Cliff, at 2 pm on a January day in 1843. A considerable number of official and unofficial spectators witnessed this pioneering use of explosives in civil engineering, made the more impressive because the firing was by electricity and the charges were deeply buried. Eyewitness accounts speak of the muffled rumbling, the vibration of the earth, and slow collapse of perhaps a million tons of chalk which rolled out into the sea in a cloud of white dust.

This area arouses thoughts of the Channel Tunnel, the great hope of the South Eastern's Sir Edward Watkin, and of the French Nord Railway's Rothschilds. Some trial borings revealed the existence of the Kent coalfield, which provided the fuel for later S.E. & C.R. locomotives and those of the Southern.

The London, Chatham and Dover reached Dover later, and by a totally different route with some notably steep banks for the trains to surmount. Both lines originally approached London circuitously for historical reasons, but a number of improvements greatly shortened the routes: notably the line from New Cross, through Sevenoaks to Tonbridge. In London, the joint committee found itself with five major stations: the through platforms at London Bridge, the termini at Cannon Street and Charing Cross, half of Victoria and the terminus at Holborn Viaduct.

The London area of this railway was an intricate network of fairly unprofitable lines carrying a large commuter traffic. The legacy of the two old companies was deplorable, especially in the matter of the carriages, which were small four wheelers mostly oil-lit and providing extremely cramped seating. The view from the window, if obtainable, was equally depressing, for this was brick viaduct and tenement country, and even the moderately well off had to gaze upon the living conditions of the London poor, on their way to small and pretty villas on the outskirts. It was doubtless an incentive to get on in the world, and this incentive was translated in practice into a move further out along the same railway, so the suburbs spread, actively encouraged by the railway management, with the result that London's commuter land is still far larger to the south than to the north.

But there was another and totally different aspect to the South Eastern and Chatham. Surprisingly, it was a railway of great style and elegance. Charing Cross was—and is—in the best position of any London terminus, and its hotel has always been excellent. The trains produced under the new management were of great beauty—the locomotives having simple and graceful lines, adorned with the most elaborate livery which gave them a sort of subdued splendour at the head of their wine-dark trains. And some of these trains were made of elaborately but delicately decorated American-type Pullman cars, while the boat trains were mostly of non-corridor compartment stock, liberally provided with lavatories and beautifully finished outside and in. The high finish was already on its way out when the Great War broke out, but it undoubtedly did much for the morale of passengers and staff, though nothing at all for the shareholders.

The luckless S.E. & C.R. commuter was also allowed a small part of this new age of elegance. Four-wheeled carriages of greater length, width and height, and more comfortable seating, were marshalled behind small tank locomotives which for some years sported the Brunswick green livery, lined out in black, cream, red and pale green, and edged with brown, like the express engines; and these too had their domes of polished brass and brass-beaded splashers. But the track and underline bridges were light, and the process of strengthening was inevitably long drawn out (in fact it lasted right through the period of Southern Railway ownership). This meant that all locomotives were small, and all trains in consequence either light or slow, and explains why the heavy vestibuled corridor carriage was not built by the S.E. & C.R. until just before the grouping.

Apart from the commuter traffic, handled at nearly a hundred stations in greater London, and the boat train passengers, the railway also handled large numbers of holiday makers in the summer months, often in old carriages not used for the rest of the year. There were resorts all the way round the Kent coast from the Thames estuary to the Sussex border, and their proximity to London made some available to the less affluent middle classes. The best that can be said of these services was that the journeys were mercifully never long, though longer than they should have been, and the fares were low—very low for some day trips, when a half-crown would buy a day at the seaside. But the S.E. & C.R. also enjoyed the prestige of carrying the Royal Mails to almost everywhere east of Great Britain—to Holland and northern Europe via Queenborough (for the Dutch boats to Flushing), to southern Europe and ultimately to India and almost all of Asia, plus Australasia, via Dover and Folkestone. Much of the traffic from these two ports was taken in the company's own steamers, of which there were usually about twenty in commission, rather more than half being passenger vessels. These ships were as fast then as they are now, but not fitted with the modern stabilisers and decidely slimmer in underwater hull shape. They were beautiful vessels, but not good for those passengers with weak stomachs, and attempts had been made in the nineteenth century to alleviate the sufferings of such people by providing a twin hulled steamer, the Castalia, and another with a swinging saloon meant to stay level regardless of the rolling of the ship. But both were failures, and the combination of rough channel weather and the speedy passage of the mails continued to make regular travellers long for a Channel Tunnel.

The locomotive history of the South Eastern and Chatham is of great interest. The two old companies had strong traditions which differed considerably. The South Eastern, with the more level road, had used Crampton locomotives, with big, lightly loaded driving wheels at the rear, and later had a notable series of 'Mail' engines designed by Cudworth. These were 2-2-2s, but generally Cudworth built 2-4-0s. He was one of the pioneers of coal firing—as distinct from the use of coke—but his system, which involved a divided firebox, was not as good as that devised on the Midland and subsequently adopted everywhere else. Just before the formation of the joint managing committee, the locomotive engineer was James Stirling, the brother of the Great Northern's Patrick Stirling. He had succeeded his brother on the Glasgow and South Western, and there adopted the 4-4-0 wheel arrangement which he continued when he came to the South Eastern in 1878. Like his brother, he preferred domeless boilers, but he was not a brilliant engineer like Patrick. His engines lasted well, some right through to nationalisation and beyond, but they never sparkled in performance.

The London, Chatham and Dover had employed William Kirtley, son of the Midland's Matthew Kirtley, as locomotive engineer since 1874. His predecessor had been William Martley, who in fourteen years had built up a good stock of sturdy locomotives all known by names rather than numbers, and in some way these names expressed defiance of the South Eastern, or boasted of the Royal Mail contract while the Chatham company had won by what must have been South Eastern oversight: not only was there 'Europa', but 'Asia' as well. The small works at Longhedge in south London could not compare with the S.E.R. works at Ashford, but by the time of the joint management Longhedge was producing the better locomotives. As both Kirtley and Stirling were of an age to retire, a very neat and successful arrangement was made whereby the S.E.R. carriage engineer, H. S.

34 One of William Kirtley's excellent London, Chatham and Dover 4-4-0s.

Wainwright, became the chief, but the actual design of locomotives was carried out by Robert Surtees, the Chatham company's chief draughtsman, who moved with his staff to new quarters at Ashford. Wainwright was a considerable artist in his designs, and applied this talent to beautifying the plain and elegant products of Surtees.

One immediate result of joint working was the introduction of new services exploiting the possibilities of the enlarged network. Unfortunately, the dropping of old services was not so immediately possible, and the result was a permanent shortage of motive power. Thus it came about that the S.E. & C.R. at various times borrowed locomotives from the Great Northern and the Hull and Barnsley (with the amusing result that its metals were used by the products of three Stirlings, two brothers and a son), and bought five small express locomotives built to the designs of William Pickersgill and originally intended for the Great North of Scotland Railway. These last brought to the railway a particular shape of cab front and splasher which was subsequently to be especially admired in the Wainwright/Surtees locomotives, of which the first appeared in 1901. Known as class D, or as 'coppertops', these beautiful and long lasting machines were only marginally more powerful than their Chatham Railway forerunners, Kirtley's class M, but the state of the railway tracks made it necessary to progress gradually. The next express passenger class, the E, was again only very slightly enlarged, and it is significant that it was worth reducing the driving wheel diameter by the small amount from 6 ft. 8 in. to 6 ft. 6 in. to save a little weight to offset the extra imposed by a slightly larger, square topped, firebox. The later addition of superheating to an E severely reduced its route availability.

These express engines, the 0-6-0 class C goods, and the 0-4-4 tanks, were all extremely good machines, and all richly adorned until Wainwright's retirement, but they were completely traditional in design. It was not until R. E. L. Maunsell succeeded Wainwright, Surtees retired, and a new team including recruits from the Great Western and the Midland took over, that S.E. & C.R. locomotive designs took a long stride into modernity.

35 A Maunsell 'Mogul' in Southern Railway colours. This design was truly modern in 1917, and scarcely less so 40 years later.

The first Maunsell 2-6-0 appeared in 1917, and showed Great Western influence in having a high boiler pressure, a tapered boiler with a Belpaire firebox, and long travel piston valves. In addition, and unlike the G.W.R., but more like the Urie designs of the L.S.W.R., it had external Walschaerts valve gear and a medium sized superheater. It was the first British locomotive to incorporate all the main features which eventually were to characterise the standard locomotives of British Railways, and a long series was built after the war and in Southern Railway days, when Maunsell was in charge of the locomotive affairs of the group. Another notable achievement was rebuilding some of the Wainwright 4-4-0s with superheaters and long-travel valves, a conversion which produced one of the most powerful British 4-4-0 types for its weight. The cleverness of this redesign was widely admired in engineering circles, not least because it gave the railway time to improve its permanent way and structures, while providing improved services in the meantime.

Before detailing the history of the South Eastern and Chatham and the two railways which together formed it, we may evoke a scene from the last year of its existence: the evening rush hour at Borough Market Junction. This place was marked by a signalbox, perhaps the busiest for its size anywhere in the world. Here trains from Charing Cross and Cannon Street pass on their way to London Bridge, and some run between the two termini. Trains for Cannon Street from London Bridge (and, of course, far beyond) have to cross the tracks of those from Charing Cross to London Bridge. There are also movements of empty stock and light engines. This place has often been a source of delays, but in the last years before the grouping a great effort at replanning the services has made a great difference, and now, in 1922, we can see 50 trains leaving London pass here, in 68 minutes—all steam hauled, all on time, and all obeying the old semaphore signals often hard to read amid the clouds of steam. Electrification and colour light signals are still in the future: engines are puffing and whistling all around.

36 Steam 'motor train' at Greenwich Park, with class P 0-6-0T.

When in 1899 the two previously rival concerns, the South Eastern and the London, Chatham and Dover Railways, were finally united, their fusion was long overdue. Indeed it could have occurred as early as 1855 when the Chatham company was still in the process of building its line from Strood to Canterbury via Chatham and Rochester, but the S.E.R. failed to seize its opportunity and much money and effort was thereafter wasted in ruinous competition.

The South Eastern Railway was the first in the field in 1836 with its proposal to build a line from the London and Croydon Railway's terminus at London Bridge to Folkestone and Dover via Oxted, Tonbridge and Ashford. In an effort to keep the number of lines into London to a minimum, Parliament sanctioned the basic plan of the S.E.R. but changed its route slightly to accommodate the London and Brighton company also being formed at that time. Instead therefore of passing through Oxted, the South Eastern was compelled to proceed south to Redhill on a line built by the Brighton but partly owned by the S.E.R. and then to turn almost directly eastwards to Tonbridge and Dover. The line was opened to Tonbridge in May 1842, to Headcorn in August, to Ashford in December, to Folkestone in June 1843 and to Dover Town in February 1844.

In addition to the inconvenience caused by the change of route, however, the congestion in London itself, with at one stage four companies (the London and Brighton, the South Eastern, the London and Croydon and the London and Greenwich) using the L. & G.R. line, made the situation almost intolerable. The London and Greenwich, in an attempt to ease the situation, had in 1842 built two additional tracks between London Bridge and Corbett's Lane but unfortunately they were laid on the wrong side of its own line, so forcing the S.E.R., the London and Brighton and the London and Croydon trains to cross the path of the Greenwich trains to reach their joint station. The only obvious solution to this problem was for the Greenwich company to exchange stations with the other three, which it did in 1844.

Further to relieve the congestion, however, the S.E.R. and the L. & C.R. in May 1844 opened their own terminus at Bricklayer's Arms and the subsequent loss of tolls for the Greenwich Railway compelled it to lease its line to the S.E.R. in 1845. This was followed in 1846 by the London and Brighton company absorbing the L. & C.R. to become the London, Brighton and South Coast Railway, so finally reducing the number of separate concerns operating from the London Bridge area to two.

While the London situation was being thus somewhat eased extensions to the S.E.R. system were under way in Kent. In September 1845, the line from Tonbridge to Tunbridge Wells had been completed and work was progressing on the Ashford to Canterbury stretch opened in 1846 to link with the Canterbury and Whitstable Railway. The Canterbury and Whitstable was the oldest section of the S.E.R., opened in May 1830 and leased by the South Eastern in 1844, but it soon lost any importance it once had as a coastal outlet route. Three lines of great value for the South Eastern holiday traffic were built to Ramsgate, Margate and Deal in 1846 and 1847 while Hastings, another promising coastal resort, was provided with two S.E.R. approaches, one via Ashford and Rye opened in February 1851 after considerable friction with the L.B. & S.C.R., and one via Robertsbridge and Tunbridge Wells opened in February 1852. The line from Gravesend to Strood laid on the bed and towpath of the former Strood canal was finally linked with London in 1849 and then came one of the most ambitious moves of the S.E.R. with its purchase of the Guildford, Reigate and Reading line. The line had been built by an independent concern but worked by the S.E.R. from its opening in 1849 and although never very flourishing it epitomised the bravado of the South Eastern in cutting straight across L.B. & S.C.R. territory and penetrating well into the preserves of the G.W.R. It was also a line of some military value linking Aldershot with the straits of Dover but at the time of its purchase several S.E.R. directors remained unconvinced of its usefulness and, taking into account other aspects of S.E.R. policy, felt obliged to resign in protest.

The major part of S.E.R. track was by this time complete and future development was confined to linking existing lines such as the Paddock Wood-Maidstone with the London-Strood, and to shortening the main route from London to Dover.

This latter became increasingly important as the East Kent Railway developed into the London, Chatham and Dover and began to rival the South Eastern's services.

The East Kent had been formed in 1853 to continue the South London-Strood line to Canterbury and so provide a more convenient route from the capital. Financially, the company was shaky and did not at first seem to present any real threat to the S.E.R. which treated it as a potential feeder for its own system. Hence when in 1855 the East Kent sought to lease or sell its line to the S.E.R. the latter declined the offer in the belief that the company would be of greater service left to shoulder its own financial burdens while still channelling its traffic onto S.E.R. track. Such was not to be the pattern though, for already an extension had been granted to the East Kent taking the original line from Canterbury to Dover, and, following the refusal of the S.E.R. to embrace the new system, further powers were obtained for an extension into London. The line was opened from Chatham to

Faversham in 1858, from Chatham to Strood in 1857 on completion of the Medway Bridge and from Faversham to Canterbury in 1860. The title of the railway was changed from the East Kent to the London, Chatham and Dover in 1859 and the two completing sections of track opened to London, St. Mary Cray in 1860 and to Dover Harbour in 1861. From St. Mary Cray, the L.C. & D. obtained running powers into Victoria station and opened its own station at Blackfriars in 1865.

From the point of view of the S.E.R. its fullscale competitor had arrived. The once quite insignificant East Kent line now had two stations, both over-shadowing the S.E.R.'s Bricklayer's Arms, and a route to Dover Harbour several miles shorter than the S.E.R. route to Dover Town. To cap it all in 1862 the S.E.R. had committed a tactical error in rejecting the Continental mail contract offered to it by the government, so leaving the way open for the London, Chatham and Dover. Conveying the Royal Mail may not have been a lucrative business but it was a prestigious one and the prestige went to the Chatham Company. Not surprisingly, the S.E.R. had been spurred to action to shorten its main route and improve its city station facilities. Under the new impetus, the Charing Cross Company, sponsored by the South Eastern to build a line from London Bridge over the river to Charing Cross, had been amalgamated into the S.E.R. and Charing Cross station opened in 1864.

A fourth S.E.R. station was opened at Cannon Street in 1866. Powers were also obtained for the S.E.R. to build a new cut-off line through Grove Park to Chislehurst, Orpington, Sevenoaks and Tonbridge and with its opening in 1868 the S.E.R. had gained a $1\frac{1}{2}$ mile advantage over the L.C. & D. route to Dover. The Chatham company had not been inactive however and between 1862 and 1866 had extended the Victoria line to Herne Hill, opened its city line to Elephant and Castle, completed the Ludgate Hill link and opened its junction with the Metropolitan Railway at Farringdon Street. Snow Hill and Holborn Viaduct stations were opened in 1874. As far as the country lines were concerned, the Kent Coast Railway, which was worked by the L.C. & D. had reached Margate and Ramsgate Harbour from Faversham in 1863 and an L.C. & D. branch line had been opened from Sittingbourne to Sheerness but the company had really taken on more than was wise and in 1866 found itself bankrupt. It took Lord Cranborne, chairman of the equally unstable Great Eastern Railway, until 1871 to sort matters out but in spite of the difficulties and in spite of its constant poverty the Chatham survived to rival the South Eastern for many years.

Indeed from the mid 1860s onwards the rivalry between the two companies was intensified by the clash of personalities, with J. S. Forbes coming from the Dutch Rhenish Railway to be General Manager of the L.C. & D. in 1861 and being promoted to Managing Director in 1871; and Edward Watkin of the Manchester, Sheffield and Lincolnshire being appointed General Manager of the S.E.R. in 1864 and two years later becoming chairman. Prospects of peace heralded by the Continental Agreement of 1865, in which the two companies agreed to share the proceeds of their continental traffic, proved illusory. There were clashes over Watkin's plan to build a channel tunnel linking Dover and Calais when, in 1883 after 2,015 yards had been bored, work was stopped for military reasons and suspicion fell on Forbes of having urged this decision on the War Office. There were further clashes between 1880 and 1884 when the L.C. & D. obtained powers to extend the 1874 Maidstone line to Ashford and when the S.E.R. opened its line to Port Victoria and began running rival steamers to Flushing. Battle raged too for many years over the S.E.R.'s refusal to pay anything to the L.C. & D. on its continental traffic worked to Shorncliffe instead of Folkestone and the L.C. & D.'s refusal to pay anything to the S.E.R. on its continental traffic from Sheerness.

There was litigation and the decision, when finally reached in 1890, was in favour of the Chatham on both counts and cost the S.E.R. £85,000.

Both companies, serving for the most part the same towns, inevitably ran competing trains, but on occasions the competition was apt to get out of hand. In 1877 for example when the S.E.R. introduced an express between London and Ramsgate known as the 'Granville Special Private Express' the L.C. & D. promptly countered it with its own 'Granville Express'. This same stubborn rivalry was evident during the Paris exhibition of 1889 with the Chatham inaugurating a special afternoon service from London with connections for Paris and calling the train the 'Paris Limited Mail' and the S.E.R. introducing a parallel service and calling its train the 'Club Train'. Both offered the best passenger comfort but both proved very unprofitable and were withdrawn in 1893.

The main business of both companies and that which kept them going during even the most difficult years, was their Continental traffic. Both did reasonably well at it and earned good reputations for their principal boat trains. The S.E.R. was the first at Dover in 1844, and ran eight trains a day from London linking with steamers to Ostend and Calais until 1862 when the L.C. & D. acquired the mail contract. Thereafter the S.E.R. transferred the majority of its continental business to Folkestone, the one time small fishing harbour, developed into a thriving port by the railway. It still ran trains to Dover, the most famous being hauled by the Dover mail singles of 1861, but henceforth the majority of its boats left from Folkestone.

The L.C. & D. Railway concentrated its fleet on Dover, its only other port being the rather minor one at Queenborough and, coming relatively late into the business, it was distinguished by its outstandingly modern steamers. For five years after the removal of the S.E.R. fleet to Folkestone the Chatham Continental service found itself taking second place to that of the S.E.R. in popular esteem because of its longer route, but following the construction of a new French line in 1867 between Calais and Boulogne, the speed of the journey to Paris via Dover was greatly increased to rival that of the S.E.R. via Folkestone. Thereafter the proportion of passengers travelling to Paris via Dover and the L.C. & D. steadily increased.

Coaching stock on both lines varied greatly, being very poor on branch lines and reasonably good on the main boat train routes. The Chatham, with the worse reputation, still managed to excel with its main line traffic, presenting in 1875 the luxurious Mann 'Palace Car' with drawing room, smoking saloon, family saloon and honeymoon compartment. Both companies introduced bogie stock reasonably early on, the S.E.R. on its Folkestone route in 1880, the L.C. & D. on its Dover route

37 A hop-pickers' special—a S.E.C.R. speciality. The second locomotive is an ex-S.E.R. Stirling 4-4-0.

in 1889, and both experimented with Pullman type vehicles, the S.E.R. running the famous 'Folkestone Vestibuled Limited' and the 'Tunbridge Wells Pullman' in the 1890s. But the usual pattern was to see coaches of 1849 still running on local routes in 1889 and later.

A wind of change was soon to be felt in both the L.C. & D. and the S.E.R., however, following the resignation of Edward Watkin in 1894. None of his successors, namely the Hon. J. Byng in 1894, Sir George Russell in 1895 and Cosmo Bonsor in 1898, had the same animosity towards Forbes and the L.C. & D. that had characterised Watkin and his administration. Consequently a closer relationship between the two concerns was soon to develop, ending in their working union in 1899. The South Eastern and Chatham Railway was born.

The Joint Committee formed to administer the pooling of resources found itself faced with numerous problems not the least of which were the overcrowded and poor track, the old rolling stock and the underpowered locomotives. A vigorous start was made in improving the entry and facilities in London with a double relief line being opened between Southwark Park and North Kent Junction in 1903 and the main line being quadrupled in 1905. London Bridge low level station was rebuilt in 1899, a flying junction was provided at Chislehurst to ease the interchange of traffic between the two companies, and Dover Marine station, which offered vastly improved passenger facilities, was opened in 1914.

With the improvement in the condition of the track came improvements to the locomotive stud. Carriages too improved in some cases, with 60 ft. Pullman cars being used on the main lines to Dover from 1910 and specially luxurious coaches being introduced for Continental traffic in 1921. These were wide spacious designs with a new type of bogie which became standard on the Southern Railway. The majority of other routes however, for financial reasons, had to make do with old stock and commuters were often subjected to particularly spartan conditions. The 'Association of Kent Coasters', a voluntary association of season ticket holders formed in 1911, was the exception. It had its own private saloons, attached to trains running to and from Ramsgate. Besides the heavy holiday and commuter traffic within its own network, the South Eastern and Chatham also made agreements with the G.N.R., the G.W.R., the L.N.W.R., the G.C.R. and the Midland enabling it to run through carriages to places such as Liverpool, Shrewsbury, Manchester, Nottingham, Huddersfield and Sheffield. Relations with the L.B. & S.C.R. however remained somewhat strained.

With the outbreak of the 1914-18 war the S.E. & C.R. had to assume heavy responsibilities for organising and running vital troop and supply trains to and from the coast. It did its job well and yet in many ways the war robbed it of the opportunity to enjoy the fruits of its labour in improving services and track. On the eve of the grouping, the S.E. & C.R. was in the forefront of modern signalling and with its reorganisation of timetables and improvements in locomotive and rolling stock had gone a long way to becoming a highly efficient concern; yet it still had not entirely thrown off the old image of the hard pressed but ruthless South Eastern and the poor but fighting London, Chatham and Dover.

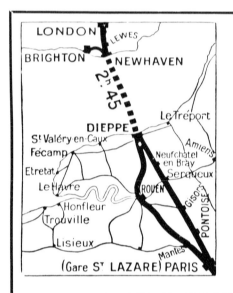

THE

SHORTEST,

CHEAPEST,

AND MOST

PICTURESQUE

ROUTE

is VIA

NEWHAVEN & DIEPPE

to PARIS and ALL PARTS of FRANCE, SWITZERLAND, ITALY, SOUTH GERMANY, AUSTRIA, SPAIN, and the MEDITERRANEAN

TWO FAST SERVICES DAILY,
Leaving VICTORIA (Brighton Railway) at 10.0 a.m., and
VICTORIA and LONDON BRIDGE at 8.45 p.m.

FREQUENT EXCURSIONS to DIEPPE, ROUEN, PARIS & RIVIERA.	**THROUGH CORRIDOR CARRIAGES** BETWEEN DIEPPE, PARIS, JURA, LAUSANNE, VEVEY, MONTREUX, UPPER RHONE VALLEY, SIMPLON, MAGGIORE, and MILAN in connection with Day Service.	**FAST SERVICES TO** RIVIERA, PYRENEES, SPAIN, LUCERNE, ENGADINE, CENTRAL SWITZERLAND, and TYROL.

DIRECT AND CIRCULAR TICKETS ISSUED TO ALL PARTS.

Through Registration of Baggage.   Baggage Insurance.

THE DIRECT ROUTE VIA PONTOISE IS NOW OPEN.

24 to 25-KNOT TURBINE STEAMERS.

Full particulars on application to—
CONTINENTAL MANAGER, Brighton Railway,
Victoria Station, London, S.W.

1913.

38 L.B. & S.C.R. Publicity, 1913

Major routes of the London, Brighton, and South Coast Railway

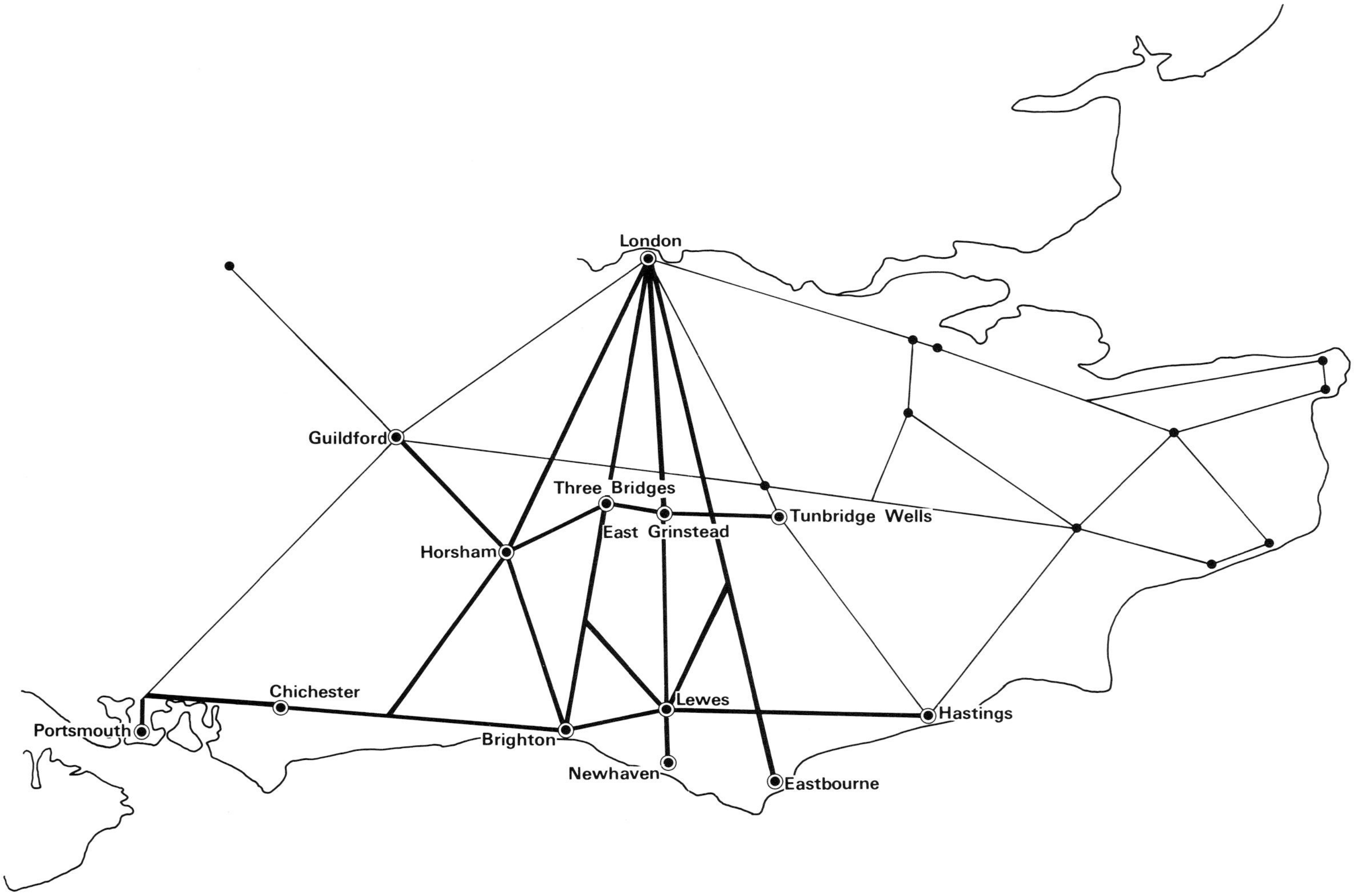

thin lines indicate other connecting railways

Hastings

Eastbourne

Tunbridge Wells

Lewes

London

East Grinstead

Three Bridges

Newhaven

Brighton

Horsham

Guildford

Chichester

Portsmouth

The London Brighton and South Coast Railway

39 The 'Southern Belle' with class H2 'Atlantic', c. 1914.

The names of British railways were always geographical and informative, if sometimes over ambitious. Some smaller railways had names which indicated aspirations rather than achievements—the Lancashire, Derbyshire and East Coast comes to mind—but in Britain there was nothing as totally misleading as the name 'New York Central', which was not an urban underground but a major trunk railway. Within the geographical form of British railway names there was still some scope for individuality and some reflection of the attitude of the directors. The great railways, whether they called themselves great or not, had names suggesting large areas of the country: Western, South Western, North Western, Northern and so on. Lesser lines made more use of the names of towns, like the bankrupt and decrepit Wrexham, Mold and Connah's Quay; or the extremely profitable and well equipped London, Tilbury and Southend. The London Brighton and South Coast was singularly well named: it was a London suburban railway which also served Brighton and nearby coastal resorts, and eventually turned them into London suburbs too.

The Brighton line was not really interested in its rural traffic, but it was obliged to do something about it, and in its middle years, before it all became suburbanised, it could be a very rural railway indeed. But the railway we can still remember had a very urban and middle-class flavour. One did not associate it with workmen's trains or coal traffic, though both existed, neither did it take dogs and guns to annual orgies of fashionable larder-stocking. Its boat trains certainly started one off for Paris (by the cheapest route) but did not carry the Royal Mails, and there were no ocean liner specials such as dignified great railways, and even the modest Tilbury line. But this unexciting railway had unexpected delights.

One of these was the show train of the line, the 'Southern Belle', which ran the 50 miles between London and Brighton in one hour precisely. Although the journey was once accomplished in 48 minutes, an hour was quite fast enough, because at the London end the tracks were tortuous. Moreover, in its great days, this was a train exclusively of Pullman cars, and one hour was the correct allowance for the civilised taking of tea, and its drinking without spillage. It was a lovely train, usually drawn by the only really large L.B.S.C. tender engine type—a Great Northern Atlantic with a more elegant and commodious cab and painted a dark brown which matched the lower sides of the brown and cream Pullmans. In later years if often had a large tank locomotive, with a name in gold letters on the tank side: 'Abergavenny', 'Bessborough', 'Charles C. Macrae'. The very last steam hauled 'Southern Belle', in Southern Railway days, was taken by one of the large tank engines bearing the name, 'Remembrance', the Brighton line's war memorial engine.

The inside of the train was even better than the outside, with very fine marquetry panelling (even in third class), expensive and comfortable upholstery, individual armchairs, and table lamps with pink lampshades. In the traditional Pullman manner, refreshments or food were served at every seat, but one was not obliged to partake of them. However, having paid the very small supplement for travelling in this luxury, one was not inclined to resist temptation.

The two London termini, London Bridge and Victoria, had little to recommend them to the ordinary passenger. For the city worker, London Bridge was only tolerable in summer, because the Thames had to be crossed to reach it, and there was no escaping the wind and rain on the bridge. Every other railway that reached London, except the Great Central, had some way of bringing its trains into the City (though L.S.W.R. passengers had to change into that company's own Waterloo and City underground). Victoria was likewise ill-sited to serve the West End (before the time of the Victoria Line Underground) and neither station possessed the slightest charm or architectural merit; London Bridge being a sprawling confusion and Victoria, after reconstruction, being pretentious and dull. Both these station sites were shared, London Bridge with the South Eastern and Victoria with the Chatham company. Though buildings and tracks of the various owners were separated, this no doubt accounted for their uninspiring quality.

By way of contrast, the terminus at Brighton, where the company was happily on its own, was delightful, and still retains much of this character today. The high roof and curving tracks of this spacious station, its buildings and the covered forecourt, all make one regret that so little of the work of the Brighton line's architect, David Mocatta, has survived. At one time the whole railway had charmingly varied stations to his designs, but they have almost all gone now.

40 A Stroudley 'Gladstone', in Marsh umber livery, tackles the bank outside Victoria station, c. 1902.

Of the through stations, that on the junction at Lewes is still one of the most enjoyable in the whole country. Below street level, the platforms lie in a fan shape, leaving wide areas of quiet concourse spanned by long footbridges. The buildings are numerous and mostly of wood, some at street level on the footbridges, and some below. Most of this is covered by glazed roofing, and bordered by the green banks of the railway cuttings, and the sun splashes here and there into this quiet, harmonious and slightly crazy wooden village. In the days of yellow steam locomotives, Lewes station must have provided a unique experience.

Another of the unexpected delights was and is the Ouse Viaduct. The L.B. & S.C.R. was not a line of major engineering works, though there were some difficult tunnels and a rather dramatic entry to Brighton. The Ouse viaduct is a major structure, but it has none of the stark splendour of the viaduct at Welwyn over which the Great Northern stormed northward, or the bleakness of Midland viaducts high in the Pennines. It is not a sudden surprise—out of a tunnel and then high over a deep gorge—such as one finds in the Alps or even at Knaresborough. In the train, the Ouse viaduct can easily pass unnoticed, and in the soft landscape of the downland it sits with the elegance of an eighteenth century folly in a large private park. It has little pavilions at its ends and is raised upon beautifully proportioned romanesque piers.

Some readers may by now be wondering how it was possible to get this far in writing about the L.B. & S.C.R. without mentioning William Stroudley. To engineers, enthusiasts and railway historians, Stroudley represents the railway's greatest claim to fame. He was mechanical engineer from 1870 to 1889, but his influence was far greater than his position on a second-rank railway might suggest. The excellence of his designs, the artistry of their detailing and the deep yellow livery, with its variously coloured lines and borders, all aroused almost universal admiration and lent great prestige to what had been the rather decrepit image of the L.B. & S.C.R.

41 Overhead wires outside Victoria in 1914. A small Stroudley tank waits in the middle.

More important is the fact that this Oxfordshire Englishman was the founder of the 'Scottish' school of locomotive design which eventually, through the influence of Dugald Drummond and J. F. McIntosh, became so widespread in the British Isles that its character still strongly marked the locomotive stock of British Railways which was withdrawn when steam operation ended.

After a short spell with the Highland Railway, Stroudley came to Brighton with Drummond in his wake, and after Drummond had been Stroudley's works manager for five years he went back to Scotland to take charge of the locomotive affairs of the North British Railway, where he very wisely built essentially Stroudley locomotives but soon added William Adams' leading bogie. Later he went to the Caledonian, and later still to the L.S.W.R., but excellent though Drummond's engines were, it was the culmination of the Stroudley/Drummond style on the Caledonian, under John McIntosh, which produced the finest and most widely imitated designs.

But the basis of Stroudley's fame was to be found on his own railway. He transformed it. On the personal level, he was helped by succeeding J. C. Craven who was generally disliked and feared, and who left behind him a stock of locomotives, most of which worked quite well, but which were of a great number of numerically very small classes, with no interchangeability of parts. The locomotives Stroudley put on the rails were effective tools for their crews, and of a small number of standard designs so carefully worked out that they were easy to keep running and spares were always available. This was already the basis of popularity for their designer, but there were other touches as well, such as the painting of the driver's name in the cab of each locomotive and Stroudley's habit of riding on his engines and listening to what the crews had to say. He was a strict disciplinarian (and the yellow paint was partly a device to ensure that engines were kept clean) but those under him appreciated this because they knew where they stood, could depend on their fellow workers, and found his severity tempered by humanity. His premature death at the age of 56 was deeply mourned and his funeral procession in Brighton was half a mile long, so great was the respect and affection felt for him.

As an engineer, Stroudley was a perfectionist. He paid extraordinary attention to details of design, being well aware that a locomotive could be kept out of service by a trivial mechanical fault as long as by something more serious. His aim was not to make maintenance easy, but to make it unnecessary, and to him 'teething troubles' with a new design would just have been a euphemism for bad design, bad materials, or bad workmanship. This philosophy of perfection was outwardly apparent in his locomotives; every line, detail and proportion of which seemed simple and inevitable. They were not at all cheap machines to build, but they were all very powerful for their size, and economical to run, while the advantages of standardisation showed in manufacture, overhaul, and allocation to duties.

He was not only a locomotive engineer. His first job on the Brighton railway was to persuade the directors that a new works was necessary, and this he duly laid out and built with the cleverest economy, reusing much material reclaimed from other railway structures. He had done something similar for the North British and the Highland railways. He designed some of the machine tools and the cranes. He soon took charge of the railway steamers and eventually designed some of the finest paddle craft ever built, which crossed from Newhaven to Dieppe in $3\frac{1}{2}$ hours—much the same time as it takes today. These steamers had his feathering paddle wheels which reduced splashing and increased the propulsive efficiency; and were driven by compound engines with fixed cylinders, the balancing of which was ensured by counterweight in the paddles. This was locomotive practice, and it produced remarkably smooth operation which helped to attract passengers from the short sea route via Calais.

Almost without exception, Stroudley's locomotives were six-wheelers. They followed the pattern set by the Stephensons' 'Patentee' in 1837, in that the cylinders were inside, and the space between the frames ahead of the centrally placed crank axle was occupied by the driving mechanism, while that behind it was occupied by the bottom of the firebox and the ashpan. The big difference was that while many designers still preferred multiple framing (with one set outside the wheels) Stroudley opted for two frames only, inside the wheels. He even applied this design to most of his tenders, giving the locomotive and tender a pleasing unity of style. Stroudley clearly gave the lead in the adoption of inside frames only, with inside cylinders, but he also took great care with cylinder design, adopting divided ports in valve chests between the cylinders (later a reason for Drummond's successes) or putting the valve chest beneath. With these and other points of refinement he transformed the 'Patentee' concept into the form in which it dominated British locomotive construction well into the twentieth century.

Very soon after arriving at Brighton, Stroudley built the first of his 0-6-0 goods

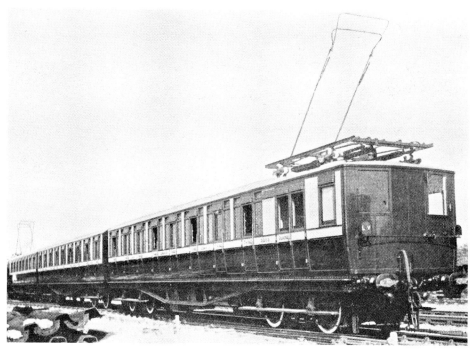

42 South London A.C. electric train set.

engines, at the time the most powerful in the country. His express engines were of two main types. First came a line of 2-2-2s, then a line of 0-4-2s culminating in the 'Gladstone' class. Both types were highly successful, but the 0-4-2 was also highly original. No other designer ever built an express engine with this wheel arrangement, and the normal thing at the time would have been a 4-4-0. But there was sound sense in what Stroudley did, because turntable lengths on the Brighton Railway at that time precluded an eight wheeled engine and tender. The orthodox solution would have been a 2-4-0, but this type commonly carried a greater weight on the leading axle than on either coupled axle. Moreover, by reversing the layout, greater freedom was allowed to firebox and ashpan, because the trailing axle was low and its position not determined by the need to couple it with rods of moderate length. 2-4-0s and 4-4-0s usually needed heavy weights at the rear to balance them, but the 0-4-2s did not—the greatest weight was on the driving wheels anyway. In the event, these engines were lighter and more powerful than their 4-4-0 successors on the railway, the Billinton B2 class, which they surpassed in every way. They also rode extremely well, and they lasted well into Southern Railway days, still working passenger trains out of Victoria in the 'twenties.

Undoubtedly the best known, best loved, and longest lived of all Stroudley's engines were the tiny 'Terrier' 0-6-0 tanks. Originally they only weighed some 25 tons, but all this was available for adhesion, of course. Built for the South London line passenger trains, these tiny machines revealed power and speed quite out of proportion to their dimensions. This was partly due to superb detail design, but was also helped by their carrying no unnecessary weight. They were all muscle, like some small athlete. Brilliant as suburban engines with four-wheeled carriages of light weight, they eventually turned out to be ideal engines for lightly laid country branch lines, and a surprising number survive to this day on preserved railways.

There was a bigger Stroudley 0-6-0 tank, used mainly for goods work, and 78 of these were built against 50 'Terriers', but the most numerous of all Stroudley's engines was the D 0-4-2 tank, of which there were 125. As already stated, the L.B. & S.C.R. was really an extended suburban railway, and a mixed-traffic tank engine could do a large proportion of the work required all over the system. The D tank could work a light express train, or a Brighton semi-fast, and it could handle all but the heaviest of the goods trains. And in quite recent years one still saw them working empty stock trains round Victoria station. Stroudley only built 32 0-6-0 tender engines, but his last design, of which only the first appeared before his death, was, significantly, a 0-6-2 tank.

The Brighton practice of putting names conspicuously on the sides of the locomotives was seen to best advantage in Stroudley's time, on his yellow livery. A 'Terrier' looked all the better with 'Tooting' or 'Piccadilly' on its side. Most of the names were of places on the railway (and the supposed confusion with destinations that this caused for passengers was the reason given for stopping the naming of engines in general) but there were such names as 'Gladstone' and many engines reminded the public of the railway's connection with the continent: one might spot 'Nuremberg', 'Lucerne', 'Toulouse', or 'Brindisi' and many others besides.

The Brighton locomotive department never reached such heights again. Robert Billinton, the next locomotive chief, built 4-4-0 express engines—poor if elegant things to begin with, but the later B4 class were good enough to earn a place beside the 'Gladstones' on the best trains. He also took Stroudley's hint and built a large number of 0-6-2 tank engines for all classes of service, which, like the little Ds, were suitable for a very large proportion of the railway's traffic.

Douglas Earle Marsh, who followed Billinton, came to Brighton from Doncaster, where he had been the works manager at the Great Northern works, under H. A. Ivatt. By this time, 1905, the L.B. & S.C.R. had some heavy coaching stock, including Pullman cars, but no locomotives suitable for pulling heavy trains at express speed. Marsh's solution was to obtain a set of large G.N. 'Atlantic' drawings from his old boss, and send them out to private locomotive building firms for tender, having marked a few alterations on them in ink. So the H1 class was born, an Ivatt 'Atlantic' with almost a Stroudley cab and a Billinton chimney, and a little later the H2 class joined it, closely similar but with large cylinders. These engines were very good indeed and were to be seen on important trains for some 45 years or more. Their last duties were on the Newhaven boat trains, just before these were electrified, and on the through trains from the North to the South Coast, the post-1945 successors to the pre-1914 'Sunny South Express'. They were the last L.B.S.C.R. express tender engines.

Still following Ivatt, Marsh produced a small 4-4-2 tank, class I1, which, though

43 The celebrated class I3 superheated express tank locomotive.

inspired by Ivatt's G.N.R. tank, was not built to the same drawings, unfortunately. It was intended to replace the D1 class, but in spite of much greater weight and size it was so inferior that Marsh had another try with class I2, which was a little better. His last attempt was class I4, the performance of which came somewhere between I1 and I2. However, among these sorry specimens there appeared a brilliant exception—class I3. This was an altogether bigger 4-4-2 tank, an express engine, using the B4 boiler. Of the first two, one was fitted with a superheater and was in fact the first British express engine to receive high superheat. This engine was compared with the L.N.W.R. unsuperheated 'Precursor' 4-4-0 'Titan' in working the 'Sunny South Express' and impressed the railway world by regularly covering nearly eighty miles without taking water, in spite of having tanks which were not abnormally large. Its performance was excellent throughout and there can be no doubt that Marsh's I3 prompted C. J. Bowen Cooke of the L.N.W.R. to create the celebrated 'George the Fifth' class, of which the first two also compared superheated and saturated steam, 'Queen Mary' being a saturated engine.

Though the I3 tanks were never the equal of the 'Atlantics' on a really heavy train, they soon found their way onto all sorts of expresses, and their tall shape still epitomised the Brighton line long after electric trains had replaced steam ones on most of the main lines. They rank as one of the great locomotive types in the history of British steam traction and one must regret that one was not preserved. Marsh's last essay in express locomotive design was class J. consisting of two 4-6-2 tank engines with outside cylinders. Their design owed much to that of the 'Atlantics', but they were rather less powerful. On the other hand, they were more powerful than the I3 class, and had a greater adhesion weight than any four-coupled locomotive, so they were well suited to working the Brighton line's fast commuter expresses and the 'Southern Belle'. They were also surprisingly lovely machines, more pleasingly proportioned than the massive 4-6-4 tanks which were their immediate successors. And they revived the old Brighton practice of bearing names. They were named 'Abergavenny' and 'Bessborough'.

Marsh's health had deteriorated badly by 1911, and upon his resignation his predecessor's son, Lawson Billinton, took charge and became the railway's last locomotive engineer. He produced the famous 4-6-4 tanks, including 'Remembrance', the war memorial engine. Most of this small group of engines only received names when they were converted by the Southern into tender engines, as a consequence of the Brighton electrification. Also in this final period there appeared one of the best of L.B.S.C. designs, the class K 2-6-0. The enginemen always claimed great things for these modestly proportioned machines, and they may have been right, because they were among the very last steam locomotives to be withdrawn by the Southern Region of British Railways.

This, then, was the locomotive history of the company (albeit told all too briefly). But a last word may be added to try to convey the total impression of Brighton locomotives, as one saw them against the buffers at Victoria, London Bridge, or Brighton—or as one saw them pulling into Newhaven Harbour or clattering round the curves and over the points into Lewes. The view of a locomotive retreating backwards from the buffers at a terminus was particularly enjoyable with the Stroudley engines, because they had tall chimneys and very large round windows in the cab fronts, the cabs themselves being rather low. They always looked very surprised at finding themselves going backwards. Somehow, this effect was not obtained on other railways. Brighton engines were tall, at least until the Southern Railway cut some of them down, and the cabs of the I3 and J classes were set high on the side tanks, and narrower, with projecting roofs over the entrances. It gave them a high collared look, and of course they were always puffing and blowing because the Brighton used the Westinghouse brake and the pump gave regular measured beats even when the engine was at rest. On the journey, as on the G.E.R., one frequently heard the pump beating frantically at stops, and when descending gradients as well.

The colours of pregrouping days are now a memory for few, but restorations in recent years have given us images of Stroudley's 'improved engine green' (actually deep yellow, but Stroudley was slightly colourblind), and of the dark brown known as 'Marsh umber'. The lining out of the former is well known but the latter deserves remark, for it was sometimes gold and sometimes yellow, while as names disappeared from the sides of tank engines they were replaced by the letters 'L.B.S.C.', or occasionally 'L.B. & S.C.R.' Engines looked well in the dark holly green of earlier Southern Railway days, with 'Southern' in bold letters on the side surmounting the number, but the later malachite tint hardly extended beyond the 4-6-2 tanks and the 'Atlantics', the best express engines, as the 4-6-4 tanks had been rebuilt, and the I3 class were relegated to secondary services.

Little has been said of Brighton coaching stock, and it was generally no more than adequate. For a time it was painted in brown and white and looked attractive enough, but Brighton line trains apart from the 'Southern Belle', rarely showed any unity of style. The roofs were either curved in a very low arc, or highly arched (giving rise to the name 'balloon stock'), and the styles were indiscriminately mixed. There might also be a solitary Pullman car, and a couple of old six-wheelers in the train, so the effect was slightly makeshift. Stroudley's stock was almost all four-wheeled, and finished in varnished mahogany, with red painted ends. Such trains showed great harmony, but were not specially good to ride in, in fact their resemblance to the stock of the North London Railway confirmed the suburban nature of the L.B. & S.C.R.

At the end of 1909, electric services began over the route between London Bridge and Victoria via the South London line—the line for which the 'Terriers' had been built. The L.B. & S.C.R., like other railways with intensive suburban services, had been badly affected by the growth of electric tramways and judged electrification of some routes to be the only way of regaining at least those passengers who were travelling three or four miles. The system adopted used alternating current at 6,666 volts, which was collected by bow collectors from overhead wires. It was soon extended to the Crystal Palace lines and their connections, and the sky outside Victoria station was darkened by a mass of substantial overhead wiring, beneath which old Stroudley engines continued to find work. In fact, many of them outlived the overhead wires, because the Southern Railway replaced them with a third rail.

The 6,666 volts A.C. system had a frequency of 25 cycles per second. It was well conceived and possibly superior to the low voltage D.C. system adopted by the L.S.W.R. and the Southern, being a sort of precursor of the 25,000 and 6,250 volts, 50 cycles, A.C. systems used in recent electrifications. After it had been supplanted, it lingered on for some years as a ghost: in the lights of London Bridge which still flickered to the old frequency.

All old Brighton line trains are now memories, and before turning to an account of the growth of the system we will give them a last look, around teatime in Victoria station, in winter, when the cold weather made the steam thicker around the locomotives and between the carriages, where the heating pipes were connected, and the hint of frost made the electric trains strike sparks from the overhead. They came in and out, these brown and white electrics, with little fuss: only a low pitched grinding of gears. A brown 'Atlantic' and a big tank engine might stand against the buffers in silence, but the small tanks on the suburban and empty stock trains made a lot of noise, most of it from their brake pumps. A Pullman train stood elegantly awaiting passengers, a glowing pink lampshade in every large window, and the crowd in the concourse was just beginning to thicken and become more agitated as the rush hour began.

Out at the platform ends, the effect was very different. All trains had to climb sharply up to the bridge over the river. Few of them were anything like as long as the platforms, so we heard them puffing loudly under the station roof as they accelerated, and when they came out into the open their white exhausts tumbled upwards into the sky. We caught a faint clanking of coupling rods and flash of wheel spokes, then the steam-wreathed train rolled by and we watched the guard's van rise towards the river with the plume of steam above it. As the engine's shouting grew fainter and was lost in the general hubbub, we heard the next train setting off under the station roof and turned to watch its emergence. For the lover of steam locomotives, the platform ends of Victoria in the evening rush hour once provided the best and most varied display in London.

Formed in July 1846 by the amalgamation of the London and Croydon line, authorised in 1835, and the London and Brighton line of 1837, the L.B. & S.C.R.

spent its early years maintaining its precarious position between the L.S.W.R. on the one hand and the ambitious South Eastern Railway on the other. It was compelled from the outset to share the line from Corbetts Lane to the terminus at London Bridge, with the London and Greenwich Railway, and the line from Norwood Junction to Redhill with the South Eastern Railway, but thence its own line ran through gentle country via Gatwick, Three Bridges and Wivelsfield to Brighton. Engineered by J. U. Rastrick the line was opened to Brighton in September 1841 where it joined the branch to Shoreham opened by the London and Brighton Company in 1840. Westwards the line was extended along the coast to Worthing in 1845, to Lyminster and Chichester in 1846 and to Portsmouth in 1847; the Havant to Portsmouth stretch being jointly owned with L.S.W.R. Eastwards the line was opened via Lewes and Polegate to the residential seaside town of Hastings in 1846. The Wivelsfield—Lewes cut off line, shortening the journey from London to Hastings, was built in 1847.

On the formation of the L.B. & S.C.R., the extent of the company's territorial claims was already marked out by this basic inverted T shaped system. The main intrusion was from the South Eastern Railway, which cut straight through its neighbours, territory with its Redhill, Tonbridge and Folkestone line of 1843 and completed the incision in 1852 by acquiring the Reading, Guildford and Reigate line. An agreement between the L.B. & S.C.R. and S.E.R. defining their respective areas of influence south of London and settling the question of tolls on their joint lines failed to prevent arguments over the proposed S.E.R. access to Caterham, Tattenham and Eastbourne, and it was to forestall further S.E.R. ambitions for entering Brighton, the very heart of the L.B. & S.C.R., that the lines to and from Tunbridge Wells were built. 1855 had seen the Three Bridges to East Grinstead line opened and absorbed by the Brighton Company, and in 1858 the branch from Lewes to Uckfield was built and the owning company bought by the L.B. & S.C.R.—quick to see the possibilities of establishing its eastward extension. Two independent companies, the Brighton, Uckfield and Tunbridge Wells Co. and the East Grinstead, Groombridge and Tunbridge Wells Co. were then encouraged by the L.B. & S.C.R. to complete the lines to Tunbridge Wells. Both companies were absorbed into the L.B. & S.C.R. in 1864 and the lines opened from Groombridge to Tunbridge Wells in 1866 and from Uckfield to Tunbridge Wells in 1868, thus securing the east Brighton approach.

Concurrently with these developments, steps were being taken to improve the access to Portsmouth and protect the western approach to Brighton in the face of possible L.S.W.R. competition. The line from Three Bridges to Horsham had been opened in 1848 and extended to Petworth by the Mid-Sussex company in 1857. The Christ's Hospital to Shoreham line via Itchingfield Junction was opened in 1861, covering the west Brighton approach. The Mid-Sussex branch joining the coast line at Arundel Junction was opened in 1860 and afforded a shortened route to Portsmouth which, although still longer than the L.S.W.R. direct Portsmouth line, was nevertheless a great improvement on the previous L.B. & S.C.R. run via Brighton. The line from Petworth was completed to Midhurst by the Mid-Sussex and Midhurst Junction Railway in 1866, while the L.B. & S.C.R. acquired the Mid-

44 Marsh's last design, the class J 4-6-2 tank locomotive. This engine was as good as it looked and gave some 40 years service.

Sussex Railway in 1862 and the Mid-Sussex and Midhurst Junction Railway in 1864, and completed the line from Midhurst to Chichester seventeen years later.

Connections to Guildford and Leatherhead, proposed originally by independent companies, were absorbed by the L.B. & S.C.R. in 1864 and the Leatherhead branch afforded an alternative route to London via the joint L.B. & S.C.R. and L.S.W.R. line to Epsom town. In London itself L.B. & S.C.R. lines served Norwood, Streatham, Battersea, Crystal Palace and Clapham Junction, and a new West End terminus, Victoria, was opened in 1860. London Bridge Station however, remained open and for many years continued to rank as the principal L.B. & S.C.R. terminus.

Branches to the coastal towns of Newhaven, Eastbourne, Littlehampton and Bognor were constructed in 1847, 1849, 1862 and 1864 respectively and the basic track network completed in 1880 by the construction of the eastern boundary line linking the joint S.E.R. & L.B.S.C.R. Croydon and Oxted line to the Eastbourne–Hailsham branch and incorporating the famous single track 'Cuckoo' line from Heathfield to Redgate Junction.

From the outset the L.B. & S.C.R. had been dependent on a high turnover of passenger traffic for the major part of its revenue. Few industrial centres lay within the compass of its lines and almost of necessity it had turned to the numerous seaside and country towns ripe for development by an enterprising railway. Hastings, Eastbourne and Worthing, Lewes and Chichester and above all Brighton were consequently the objects of concerted railway promotion. Londoners were encouraged to visit the coast or to live in the country at such places as Reigate, Dorking, Horsham and Tunbridge Wells and travel to work by the railway. Commuters were early enticed to the healthier clime of Brighton by the appearance of first class season tickets in 1844 and the announcement in 1851 of a $1\frac{1}{4}$ hour train service. By 1865 Brighton had become the haven of many wealthy business men travelling to and from their offices by what was to become the famous 'City Limited' leaving Brighton at 8.45 a.m.

Portsmouth traffic, after the completion of the L.S.W.R. Direct Portsmouth line, was run in competition with the L.S.W.R. but in spite of the South Western's shorter route, the Brighton Company almost managed to equal the L.S.W.R. timings from London. Furthermore it had sponsored the development of Newhaven as a port and under the guise of the Maples and Morris Company had begun operating steamers to Dieppe in 1847. By 1862 it was running a joint steamer service with the French Western Railway and offering its passengers the shortest route to Paris, London to Paris via Dieppe being only 257 miles, as against 259 miles for the Folkestone–Boulogne route and 286 miles for the Dover–Calais route. Steamers from Littlehampton ran to St. Malo in 1867 in competition with the L.S.W.R., and from Portsmouth to the Isle of Wight in conjunction with the L.S.W.R.

The extent of the L.B. & S.C.R.'s reliance on its excursion and commuter traffic was evident during the financial crisis of 1867 when a fall in the passenger receipts brought the company to the verge of bankruptcy even though its goods trade had done well. Accordingly it was in terms of passenger train economy that the recovery was affected. Samuel Laing, chairman of the company from 1867 to 1898, and J. P. Knight, general manager from 1870 to 1886, reduced the number of passenger train miles covered by the railway and introduced cheaper fares for both excursionists and commuters to encourage intensive use of its trains. Revenue was soon on the upturn and by 1875 the railway was re-established as a prosperous concern. The goods trade (amounting by 1910 to $1\frac{1}{2}$ million tons of merchandise and 3 million tons of minerals) always managed to remain unobtrusively in the background. Market garden produce from the Worthing district, foodstuffs entering Newhaven from the Continent, marine supplies and heavy goods handled at the Deptford and Battersea yards somehow failed to disturb the aura of this predominantly passenger line.

Printed in England for Her Majesty's Stationery Office by
Staples Printers Kettering Limited, The George Press, Kettering Northamptonshire

Dd 587539 K96